FROM PAIN TO GAIN
"THE LIFE OF A LITTLE JAMAICAN GIRL FROM ST. ANDREW"

AVIS S WILLIS

From Pain to Gain
The Life of a Little Jamaican Girl
From St. Andrew.

Copyright © 2021 by Avis Willis.

All rights reserved. Printed in the United States of America. No part of this book may be used or reproduced in any manner whatsoever without written permission except in the case of brief quotations embodied in critical articles and reviews. Permission granted on request.

Qui 2 Life Publishing
34 Shining Willow Way
LaPlata, MD 20646
www.qui2life.com
1 (301) 710-5219

Paper cover ISBN: 978-1-7326177-4-2

eBook ISBN: 978-1-7326177-5-9

Library of Congress Cataloging-in-Publication Data

Name: Avis Willis

Title: From Pain to Gain: The Life of a Little Jamaican Girl from St. Andrew

Edited by Tonitta Hopkins and Alexis Dobbins

Cover Artwork by Aniqua Ava

Cover Design by SPJ Graphics

Qui 2 Life Publishing is not responsible for any content or determination of work. All information is solely considered as the point of view of the author.

Scriptures taken from Holy Bible, New International Version®, NIV® Copyright ©1973, 1978, 1984, 2011 by Biblica, Inc.® Used by permission. All rights reserved worldwide.

DEDICATION

I want to dedicate this book to those who have been downtrodden, broken-hearted, homeless, experienced loss in any form, and those living in fear instead of faith. Every situation requires a decision - just remember God is always with you.

ACKNOWLEDGMENTS

I want to first acknowledge God who is the head of my life. My children, Naomi, Majesty, Chosen and Dominion who gave me a purpose to do this work. To my late husband Douglas Wych II whose knowledge, encouragement, and love pushed me every step of the way. He contributed a lot of inspiration towards this book. It was his desire that I let the world know more about my culture and my testimony of how God is faithful in all his ways.

To my coach, T. Lynn Tate, I am forever grateful to you for your time and investment on this project, "my big baby." Anique Ava, your artwork for the cover of this book is exceptional. You were on point with every detail. I appreciate and celebrate your work with deepest gratitude.

Then I'd like to save the best for last. I could not have done any of this without my late parents, Hubert (The

Lion) and Merlita Willis. These two deposited strength, courage, and perseverance in me, and I am so humble and grateful for them as I carry out their legacy. Thank you, thank you, thank you!

P.S. I want to thank myself for not giving up on me and this dream.

CHAPTER 1

St. Andrew

*A*vis Stacy-Ann Willis born October 6, 1975. A little girl born in the hills of East Rural St. Andrew, Jamaica, West Indies, to the proud parents of Hubert Nehemiah Willis and Merlita Cynthia Willis. I was privileged to be born the youngest of 14 pickney, or as you would say in the United States children, 12 which were still living two which passed shortly after birth. Like my siblings, I was born at home. Although some babies were born in the public hospital in Kingston, it was far away from home with very limited transportation. There was less than three percent of the population who were car owners. Whether morning or night, going into labor came with the hardest decision. Where to have the baby? Maybe that is why the majority of the children in the community were born at home with midwives present.

My parents never told me the story of how and what time they traveled to give birth to me. It seems as though everything was kept a secret especially being pregnant. Very few people would know this until either you were coming from or going to the hospital with that newborn; or the day that child was being christened at the local church -- then it was a big thing. As I got older and my memories served me well, the only time I knew there was a baby anywhere was looking at the pastel baby clothes or cloth diapers which were referred to as "nappy" blowing on the clothes lines in the front of the house. It never sparked any questions because every household had a husband-and-wife team. It was just a quiet topic, and the clothing they wore probably hid their stomach for the length of time anyway. So being born into this family was probably a highlight.

Who would have expected the Willis family to have another child after all those earlier siblings? Here I was, tiny with high complexion, lighter than my siblings, full head of straight, shiny black hair entering the home of Mr. and Mrs. Willis, known to the community as Mas Jiggs and Ms. Merle. Stacy-Ann was given to me by my aunt, my mother's sister. I don't know why; maybe she figured my mother ran out of names (laughing). And this is where the root of my story all began.

My mother, affectionately known as "Bow," bears the title of the "Strongest and Greatest mother ever." After bearing 14 children, which included three multiple births, she called me her "wash belly" because I was her last child and "Stee," short for my middle name, Stacy. There was a little old neighbor up the hill, probably the oldest person in the community, who used to call me "bright eyes" because my eyes were so bright with a smile that represented the sunshine. So, as you can see, I had a few nicknames which were cute and made me feel special. Now in the spirit of my strong Jamaican roots, I will occasionally use Patois, which is a mixture of broken English and various West African dialects used in Jamaica. Come, let's take a walk up the hills of Mt. Hybla, St. Andrew, Jamaica. A place you might not see on the country's map, but on the map of one's memory or experiences.

There it was, the bright yellow and blue brick house with its zinc roof sitting on top of a steep hill, filled with chatter, laughter, and love. Looking at the house, the paint stripping from the previous year seemingly gave it a third color. It was customary for the house to be painted every year around Christmas, but it was not yet time. It was not a bother to anyone because there was something special, real special, about the family that lived there. It seemed as if that family was a community all by themselves. There were so many people of different complexions, shapes, and sizes living in that one house. The little yard space looked dangerous to play in because of how it was situated on the edge of the field facing down the steep rocky hill. A crooked piece of stick held up a wire clothesline that stretched across the front of the yard with clothes of all sizes and colors blowing in the brisk breeze from the surrounding trees. The sun pelted down from 6:00 am all the way to 6:00 P.M. drying those clothes faster than the wind. All the freshness of those clothes stained my nostrils as I gazed at the silver wash pans still filled with water, more clothes, and sheets in the center of the yard. The smell of homemade meals wafted from the makeshift fireplace in the backyard as the smoke penetrated the sky.

Music lingered from the tiny brown radio filled with static. It had one station, and a piece of wire hanger served as its antenna to hold up the signal. The barking of the family dogs and the purring of the fluffy cat resonated in my ears. My mother's voice periodically hailed from the back of the house calling for her children. She moved about humming her favorite gospel hymn. I watched as she blew the ashes to keep the fire blazing in the fireplace while preparing the many delicious meals that I'd hoped to learn how to make when I grew up. A tiny chicken pen sat opposite her with several chickens clucking away not knowing their fate, as one would become Sunday dinner. The clear picture of her in her long floral dress and her headwrap will be the image always I carry with me.

As I played in the yard with my make-shift doll created from a well-sucked mango seed, in the small batch of grass by the upper side of the house, the man I called

"Dada" approached me. With the strength and breadth of a strong man, he huffed up the rocky road with his black dirty rain boots, machete, and farmers bag over his shoulders. The sweat from his brows only indicated how hard he must have been working or walking those rocky roads. My father had many nicknames, but the one that stood out the most was "Lion." The vibration from his voice was so strong when he would call my name. I looked to him as my protector and hoped one day I would be blessed with someone like him with his strong characteristics to protect me just the same.

Life in Jamaica was rough and hard, but we were always peaceful and happy.

I am not ashamed to say, in the words of my late father, "We were one of the poorest families on the hills of East Rural St. Andrew."

However, that did not stop me from being the happy, pleasant, and inquisitive little girl that strived for excellence. I started reading from an incredibly young age which I believe was passed down from my father; and the fact that all my siblings were already in school by the time I was added to the family was more reason to try and play catch up to them. My father was brilliant.

He used to say, "I could read from a very young age which I believe was a gift from God."

Many days my father would sit down with books, cut out articles, and sometimes newspapers to assist his children in the reading process. As much as we were reading, we practiced our writing skills just the same. Oftentimes we had to share pencils, and when the point of any of them broke my father would get a knife and sharpen those pencils to perfection.

"The dullest pencil is better than none," he would say when the point of our pencils was getting dull.

My dad's handwriting was so neat and excellent, so he did most of the writing of grocery lists or letters exchanged locally or foreign. As far as I can remember, and even now, my sibling's handwriting is impeccable, but none can top my father's.

I always wondered what my dad would have become if he had an opportunity other than being a farmer. He often shared that during childhood there were no basic schools in the community. There was the Hall's Delight All Age School, which catered to all the children from seven to fifteen years old. So, early education was taught in the home. As for me, by the time I was born and ready for school there was a Basic School, and I had the opportunity, unlike my dad, to start my schooling at the age of two. Then I was blessed to attend the very same All Age School as my dad and was taught by some of the best teachers that took their time and taught us everything we needed to learn.

Two teachers that stand out clearly in my mind are Mrs. Carmen Wilson and Ms. Elaine Morse. They were very amazing and exercised such patience with their students. To this day, I believe they were influential in many decisions I made towards my success. These two teachers took time to impart knowledge and made sure I learned the basic skills that would make me who I am. Ms. Elaine Morse was the Basic School teacher and she lived on the upper side of my house. Whenever she was leaving for school in the mornings, it was her priority to stop by my gate and yell for my mother to bring me to her. Imagine traveling back and forth to school with your teacher. It would seem as if she was a babysitter, or better yet, a bodyguard to me because I was only two years old and would spend the next two or three years at that school.

There was no way for me to misbehave even if I wanted to, and I'd better learn what she taught me, too. If not, somehow that news would get home to my mother before she dropped me off. It might sound a little bit off that I traveled back and forth to school with my teacher, but there was a particularly good side to it. I was able to practice my school lessons with her coming home, so I had no reason to complain walking back and forth with her. It also helped that she was my Godmother, which was even more reason for me to walk with her daily. Being the brilliant man he was, my dad every evening would question what I learned that day in school. It was like he was a teacher and I a student when I was with him.

Going off to All Age School, "Big School" is what we called it, was a different setting. Big School had a bigger school yard, bigger classrooms, more teachers, and bigger students. Although my Godmother would still accompany me, I was now in the company of my older siblings. I was already known by the time it was my turn to go to Big School. For one, all my siblings were there, and I had met a lot of the students on the road while attending Basic School. The community was just rich in humility and respect and everyone knew everyone's family. You see, teachers in those days did not joke with teaching and discipline. You would be disciplined for punctuality, improper uniform, and not knowing a bible verse during daily devotion which usually took place for about an hour in the school yard with the morning sun pelting down on your head. We would escape the sun and have devotion inside only on rainy days, which were not so often.

I recall running to school on the rocky roads racing my siblings with both anticipation and fear. The Principal would be waiting at the school gate with a belt in his hand to whip anyone who was late. Just seeing his stern face intimidated me. He was thick in body with a very dark complexion, and he never had a smile on his face. You could see him standing at the school gate twirling the leather belt in his hand as he checked his watch and looked in all directions for students who were late. When I say late, I mean even one minute late was considered late with no excuses. I remember that belt as if it was yesterday and how it hurt so bad the day I became a victim to it.

One morning I came to school late, and as I got closer to the school gate, I could see his face ready to whip me. My God, my heart raced with fear feeling the sting from the belt in his hand before it even touched me. Every student that came late had to form a line, and nobody wanted to be in the front of that line.

There was one that said, "Betta yuh get first lick and yuh can cool off, then wait for last."

I thought better to not be in that line at all.

In his deep voice, the Principal would say, "Stretch out your hand."

Every slap from that belt was in the middle of your hands. There were a few real unruly students who would get a couple over their backs because they refused to stretch out their hands for that spanking.

On the day I got my spanking, I took the advice of that crazy person and I stood in front of the line, my complexion changing color and my heart pumping. Somehow, I believe my blinks lasted a bit longer as I stood before the Principle.

He said, "You are late. I saw your father earlier, so you had no reason to be late. Now, stretch out your hand."

As I held out my right hand and winced at the harshness of the belt coming towards me, I shifted my hand several times which was never a good thing because it meant I would be standing in front of the principal longer and he would increase the lashings. On several occasions the Principal got mad because the belt ricocheted and hit him. I wanted to laugh at him when it happened and ask him how it felt, but I knew better. The very few days that I was late, those lashings in my hands would cause my hands to be sore as I went off to class. The difficulty of trying to soothe the pain often distracted me from learning my school lessons, but one of the worst distractions would be a student still crying in the classroom long after they received their lashing. Sometimes they would cry so hard snot would bubble out their noses. I don't know why but that was the funniest thing to me.

Every student had an assigned single desk attached to a metal chair. If the classroom was a bit loud even from shuffling around, the Principal would sneak up and just stand by the door twirling that belt in his hand, daring any student to move. Anyone thinking that they were big and bad was going to feel that belt speaking to them. I knew to pay attention to my teacher; or at least pretend if I must, because I did not want a friendship with that belt. No one, and not me for sure, wanted to get a lashing/spanking twice in one day or week.

There was a lot of excitement during my school days at Big School. One of the most enjoyable times was Sport Day. During Sport Day all the schools in the community came together to show their talents in various sports activities. My favorite was track and field. The love for running and winning was embedded in me possibly from the two miles I had to run from my house to school daily. Even when my school did not come in first place, those moments of competition helped me feel like a winner. Those days were amazing. Then we had recess. Yes, this was another favorite. All you wanted to hear was that metal bell ringing at 11am. Every student dashed out of the classroom as if they were suffocating and in need of air.

The race began for those who played hide and seek, "Stucky, Dandy Shandy," and cricket. Recess would last for about 45 minutes. Students would come back in the classrooms with their uniforms unraveled, hairdos sweated out, some sweaty and smelling, and some late for class. It was amazing that no one fell asleep after all that "ramping." Instead, it seemed as if all that playtime gave extra energy to all of us. We were more alert to learn our afternoon lessons and eager for the sound of the lunchtime bell.

Connected to the back of the school was a building that served as our canteen. This would be your lunch spot with one of the most pleasant ladies that prepared and served lunch daily if you were not going home for lunch. She was beautiful, short in stature, and chunky. She served every child with a smile. We would line up with our bowls in hand and stand by the tiny wooden canteen window handing her our plates. Then we'd walk to our respective classrooms to eat our meal which included chicken back, white rice, and sometimes thick cornmeal porridge sweetened with condensed milk and sugar. We were responsible for washing our plates afterwards from the little pipe in the back of the school. Whenever that pipe was over-crowded, we had to travel along the road to "tank" which was a bigger pipe.

The water volume at "tank" was much better and helped those students to wash their bowls cleaner. Then we would tuck the bowl away in our bags and bring it home to bring again the following day. Those days at Big

School will always be considered my stomping grounds. It contributed to many of my childhood memories, and I will always cherish them to tell my children and generations to come.

"If your childhood does not create precious memories make sure your adulthood will." ~Verona Willis-Brown.

CHAPTER 2

Learn Your Lesson

My parents who were farmers made sure there was no lack of anything. We were surrounded by acres of land. My father got the nickname "Lion" because he was quiet, but when it came to providing for his family, he roared like a lion at any cost to meet their needs. He also could have gotten the name from the number of children he had. My father had the most children in our little community; and yet, we did not suffer or lack in any area of our lives.

My father planted coffee, one of many crops in St. Andrew. Our little yellow and blue house sat above acres of coffee plants and was surrounded by various fruit trees such as mango, oranges, papaya, peach, guava, lime, and pear. I can remember standing at the side of the house watching my parents in the coffee field toiling and laughing with each other. You never knew what they were talking about, but their smiles and laughter told it all. They were happy and full of contentment. My mother's face would light up and it would make me smile too. She had such a beautiful smile and caring eyes that would tell you how much she loved you.

The far end of the house had what you called a "pit toilet" because there was no running water to have the luxury of a flushable toilet. Then there was a brick kitchen adjacent to it where all the sumptuous meals were prepared. This was a kitchen that used wood, bushes, or small pieces of sticks to create a fireplace. Then there was one big brown container, which was called a water drum, to hold all the cooking water. It was just for the kitchen, and it was one container my mother wanted to make sure was always filled.

My mother would have her wooden table filled with all her ingredients. The food containers were tightly sealed with flour, sugar, yellow cornmeal, salt, and powdered milk also known as "milk powder." The table was small, yet she created a space there to share meals with her children. Mother was a chef, not professionally or certified, but a great cook and caterer. Talking about great cooks, I dare not leave my dad out. He barely cooked; but when he did, good heavens it was so little in serving yet so tasty leaving you swallowing your spit over and over.

When it was time to eat, our "basins," or bowls is what you would say in America, would be lined up with our spoons in them waiting for my mother to call us. As I mentioned, there were 14 children all together, but at no point did all of us live in the same house at the same time. By the time I was born, most of my elder siblings were already grown and moved out living in Kingston.

Many days I would watch my mother bent over the fireplace as she tried to ignite the fire, especially at dinner time. She would blow the smoking wood several times to fuel the flames as she placed two pots on the now blazing wood. Most of the time the smoke would burn her eyes, and she would just walk away for a quick minute only to return to her pots once her eyes were clear. I would sit in the smoky kitchen watching as she measured the rice with a small cup, or the flour with just the palm of her hand to make dumplings. Of her two pots, one was for the meat she would prepare, which would most likely be on Sundays or a couple times during the week. It was not because she did not have the resources. There was plenty of livestock there, but it was her choice to feed us vegetables most of the time.

There were only seven siblings in this three-bedroom house. My dad built this house and carried every brick by hand. You might say, "That sounds like a big house." Well in my eyes it was not. My parents and eldest brother each had a room all to themselves, and the rest of us shared one room adjusting ourselves on two beds. Nighttime was always chaotic. It was always a rush to see who would reach the bed first to get the comfortable spot in the corner, knowing if you were on the edge of the bed most likely you would fall off. I was very slender, so either way I would fit, but of course I did not want to fall off the bed at no time during the night. Sometimes it would get uncomfortable in the bed because one sibling would pee the bed, another would have dirty smelling feet, or I would just get squished. However, we made the best of it and tried to get enough sleep.

Before we fell asleep, we would tell "duppy," or ghost stories, and I would get scared and pull the cover over my head telling my brothers to stop. One thing I learned for sure was to pee before I went to bed because after those stories no one wanted to get up during the night. It was total darkness and the sound of crickets and wind blowing on the outside would get me scared even more. There was a "pee pan" or "chammy" under the bed. Even though the "pee pan" was right there, those nights when I got the urge to pee, I had to wake one of my siblings to follow me just to the foot of the bed.

Getting up every morning whether for school, church, or just a regular day was one of the most disorderly times. We had to gather water in pails to bring in the house and wash down our bodies. Did I say water? I meant freezing water where sometimes our backs didn't get washed because we wanted to hurry up and get all that cold water off us. There always seemed to be a water problem. So many days there was no water at home, and we all had to rush to the nearby water pump down by "tank," which was down the rocky route to school. We'd fetch the water and hurry back to wash up and get ready for school.

Since time was always against us, we had to hurry. Coming back with the water containers which were carried by my older siblings on their heads, we'd bump into students already going to school, or farmers on the way to their farms. By the time we got home, some of the water had spilled leaving my siblings with much less water to bathe. Being the youngest, I got to carry a jug, so my water was secured.

My mother was already in the wooden kitchen making breakfast by the time we got back from fetching the water. On most days breakfast would be the same thing: fried eggs, fried plantains, fried dumplings, or fritters with one slice of bread, and a cup of hot cocoa, tea, or natural bush tea like mint, fever grass, or leaves from the orange tree. Each one of us would get dressed in our uniforms and listen for my mother to call us one by one for our plastic basin and cup.

The good thing about getting dressed for me was one of my older sisters would do my hair on Sunday night. It was one less thing I had to worry about. My hair was neat, nice, and expected to last for the whole week; however, I had a good length of hair and liked to play in it. I'd pull out all the braids coming from school by Monday evening. My sister was not living at home with us and only came to visit on the weekends. So, I would show off the curly effect from my unraveled braids the rest of the week.

One day I had to do homework with my eldest sister; yes, the same one who did my hair. She quizzed me on spelling words. She chose the biggest word I have ever seen and will always remember, "Mississippi." Oh my God, what kind of word was that? She would slap on my hand every time I spelled it wrong but looking at the word was intimidating. All those letters across the page almost left me tongue tied.

"Spell it," she would yell, "M-I-S-S-I-S-S-I-P-P-I."

Can you believe I am still having trouble spelling it; or maybe it was traumatic, and I am having a flashback? My head hurts just with the thought of it. I am truly telling you for a week she would pound my brain with that one word as if there was no other word in the world.

One Sunday evening while she was doing my hair, she asked me to spell the word again, and every time I slipped up, she would slap me in my head with the comb.

As I tried to cry, she would tell me "Yuh betta nuh mek one eye water roll down your face."

My sister near my age would always try to rescue me. Since she was next in line to get her hair braided, she would be sitting not far from me trying to whisper the spelling of the word, hoping I would read her lips and spell it correctly.

My older sister yelled, "Nuh tell har, mek she spell it herself."

Eventually I got it and all that slapping in my head or on my hand was naught thereafter.

Most homework was done outside on the doorway or

on the verandah on an extra brick or box. Our yard was not big, yet we had space big enough for us to play different games which included hide and seek, jump rope, marbles, jigs, and whatever else we made from cardboard boxes and stitches. In the back of the brick kitchen, with its little wooden half sturdy door, we had a pig pen with two pigs. They were so pretty and even had names. To be honest, I believe all the animals at my house and everyone else's had names. Then we had several goats next to it; and above all that, was the massive soil filled with different vegetables and ground food such as potatoes, yams, and yucca. We also had tall banana trees that swung above the soil.

One of the most beautiful things would be the sunrise at the front of the house as it peeped upwards from the back of Blue Mountain Peak, the highest peak in Jamaica. The warmth of it would energize you in such a way it left you speechless at its beauty among the slightly foggy mountain. The visibility of the sun was so near, yet so far, and an amazing sight to see. Then looking at the array of flowers my mother would plant almost daily in front of the house would just beautify the place even more. There were so many flowers planted that she often took them to the market and sold them. She loved flowers so much all her clothing had floral patterns.

As much as my dad said we were the poorest family, it never seemed that way because we never lacked anything. We would wear "hand me down" clothes and shoes, but we never once cried out of not having. If anything, I believe we had more than most people because my mother always attended to someone else's child. I recall seeing other children at our house almost every day. They would have dinner, watch television, and then go home. So, if we were the poorest, then there had to be someone else lacking something more that caused them to visit our home. It could seem we were poor because we had less material things, but I strongly believe we were rich in love and respect.

Even until this day, there was no question that everyone in the community had such high respect for my parents. To some, my dad was "Lion" to others he was "Mas Jigs," which was a name given to him because he loved dancing. In his younger days, before I was born, there was a famous dance called "Jiggy." My dad mastered it, so "mas" short for "master" and "Jigs" for "Jiggy," there you have my dad the dancer. The community and others called him the "Father of Dancing," and whenever he hit the dance floor, he was the center of attraction. When you look at how my dad raised his family it was like a mark on his children. We received the same respect anywhere we went. It was not hard recognizing us. We all had a slight resemblance to my parents, so as soon as we left the house and hit the road, "A Mas Jigs pickney dat," someone would exclaim.

My father believed in having integrity, so his disciplinary actions at home were very strict, and mother had no problem enforcing them when he was not around. Oh, she would use anything and everything in her reach to slap those who were misbehaving including pots, shoes, a comb, a brush, a broom, a mop, or even her common scarf on her head.

She would then tell them, "Wait until Jigs come."

I always avoided misbehaving because I did not want to get slapped by her or my dad, but there was that one time. The thought of it makes me laugh now. Good grief there is always that "one time." That was the time I got slapped by my mother because of my mischievous brother.

The sun pelted, school dismissed, and as usual we headed up the road, and the ramping started from the time we left school to the gate of our yard. We stopped and picked jackfruit from someone's farm, picked plums and berries, and played hide and seek with no care in the world or the value of time. What was worse, we did not once notice the sun setting in the western sky, knowing once the sun started to set it was close to 5 P.M.

Someone questioned, "Jesum piece a wat time now?"

Another replied, "Bow a go kill we."

We were late coming from school. After we realized the darkness, my sister, brother, and I mounted up the rocky road to the house in such a speed as we took the long way. We could have taken the short way, but once its dark that was never a good idea. Something told me it was not going to be a good evening.

As soon as all three of us stepped into the front yard, there she was hands on her broad hips and no smile on her face. We did our regular, "Good evening Bow," as she was affectionately called. She suddenly shoved up her mouth in the air, and sucked her teeth.

"Is weh yuh saying Good evening bout, yuh know a what time now?"

We all fumbled with our words and shuffled as we pushed each other in front to face her. The thought of getting a good slap stretched across my mind real quick. I felt a warm rush from my inside, my light complexion immediately turned red, and my heart pumped hard across my bony chest. Everything happened so fast, as mother stood there and huffed. Her words were so blunt as they traveled out her mouth in slow motion.

"Go get a piece a switch, oonu think me a play dis evening," and that was the moment of truth.

My complexion got flushed as my brother pushed me in the front and dashed down the road leaving me trembling. I took a couple steps backwards as I tried to be obedient to her commands, broke off just a small whip from the little tree in my reach, and brought it to her. Oh my God did I get a whipping that evening. One I will never forget, and can you believe my brother and my sister did not? So, you must be wondering what happened to my sister, the same one who tackled those boys. Well, she created a whole scene, threw herself on the ground and bawled bloody murder without even getting one slap from mother. She was always so extra, but her extra was not in a bad way. Maybe she was crying for the both of us.

She was so extra with her bawling. She rolled on the ground and hollered in such a terrible way. You should have seen her chunky-self hollering. It was painful. After I got a couple good slaps across my arms and legs with my own little whip, mother looked down on my sister, and sucked her teeth.

She said, "But a wat smatta wid yuh, me would a like to know a who a go wash dat uniform you rolling on the ground in?"

After all that good ole whooping, my brother was nowhere in sight, and my sister barely got up as I sniffled behind my mother and went into the house.

Nightfall came upon us and my sister stood on the ground still crying. After washing up I stuck my fingers in my mouth wondering if my sister was coming inside. I peeped outside from the clear glass windows by the door and noticed she was headed back down the rocky road away from the house calling for my brother. Those two were like Tom and Jerry, when one moves the other follows. I guess she decided she was not coming in the house unless my brother was beside her. Well, it was dinner time and as I sat around the table, she came in the front door and started crying again. I guess she was hungry or maybe tired of crying and waiting for her partner in crime. Mother sucked her teeth again.

Looking at my sister she said, "Yuh lucky."

That "yuh lucky" was a way to say she wasn't going to be bothered with you, and that was the sweetest sound to my sister's ears because that only meant she was not going to be whooped.

My brother didn't come home until it was time for

bed. He came knocking on our room window whispering our names to open the door. At this time, my father was already home, had his dinner, and there was no question that mother had told him what had happened. My father had the tendency to sit around the table until sleep took him. The dinner table was literally a breath away from our room, so if we sneezed or whispered, he would be the first to hear us. Of course, Dada heard my brother calling us to open the door.

"Nuh open no door mek him tan out deh," he said.

I felt so sorry for my brother, for one it was cold and dark, and he was very much afraid of the dark. The sound of him moaning by the door and the dogs barking at him had me so worried. I really wanted to open the door. So, one of my brothers and sister constructed a plan to wait for dada to fall in a deep sleep, then one would watch him from the room door while the other took time to open the door.

So many attempts failed because of the squeaky door and sudden cool air that would flash past us making dada shift out of his sleep. Finally, my brother made it inside. You could never put anything past my parents. Their spiritual awareness was spectacular. Just as my brother snuck in the bed, my other brother had to build a wall of extra clothes on the bed to hide him as my father came in the room to check on us. We all pretended to sleep just from the sound of the chair pulling away from the table. Oh my God, we were saved. He never noticed my brother in the bed, or maybe he did and pretended he didn't so he wouldn't have to whoop him in the night. However, my father caught up with him the following day and tore his little tail up.

Sometimes you have to pretend not to see things, so things can take its course. We can call that wisdom. Even though my brother had abandoned me for the first time earlier that evening, I always felt protected when I walked with him on the street. It felt as if he had a shield of protection over me from everyone, like a serious bodyguard. I love my brother so much and thank him for that. It was only concluded that was the treatment you received when you were "the last child," which left me feeling guided and protected by everyone and everything. But life would have me to develop my own survival muscles and independence.

My mother, Bow, which was a name she earned from her younger siblings, was the Lioness. She was a dedicated mother and wife. I recall eating three meals a day, but the one that sticks with me was lunchtime when we did not eat the school lunch. That was midday when the sun was in the middle of the sky. My siblings and I had to walk up the rocky road only to get home to a hot bowl of cornmeal porridge with two slices of buttered bread. This was literally almost every day. Some days mother would still be at the fireplace when we got there, but she insisted that we waited for that porridge to be finished and cooled. We'd eat some and rush back to school without being late. As I mentioned earlier, the principal was always at the school gate waiting with his belt to deal with any students who were late.

I would try to eat as many spoons from my porridge as I could, and then rush back down the rocky road. If I fell, there was no question, I had to hurry and get up and continue to school. There was no going back home for us. It was get to school, even if we had to cry all the way there. The point was not to be late. Many days we would race each other. The slowest ones would take short cuts, while others took a regular route. I was not among the fastest, but I could run and those "short cuts" did not help me. I fell more than I ran. There were gullies I would slide down, barking dogs from the neighbors I would run past, but I never gave up. By the time I made it to school my uniform was soiled, but I made it on time.

CHAPTER 3

Bow

I often sat in the banana field and ate ripe bananas which overflowed. For every section of the farm, there was an abundance of banana trees. The orange and pear trees were right next to the house, so I just helped myself whenever I felt like eating or was waiting for my dinner. Mother was a quiet, spiritual giant and an awesome businesswoman. I remember watching her in the hot sun during the week farming and planting a variety of flowers, herbs, and spices. Then on Thursday morning she would catch the market truck to go sell her crops.

The market truck was way smaller than a trailer in size. The backend was wooden with ropes across the back to act as a door or barrier. Market goers would sit either on their bags of goods or one of the wooden benches that stretched down each side of the truck bed. It would be packed like sardines with wives and sometimes children going to sell their crops. We never got the opportunity to travel to the market with our mother.

Mother would start preparing on Wednesday. She'd reap her crops, wash them, then tie them up into small bundles ready for sale. Her dedication was just above and beyond words, and of course we were involved in every way possible. No one was too young to help. If it was just to pour a cup of water, we were going to be a part of the Willis family team. The smell of all the fresh crops in the house was amazing and tempting too, especially the fresh clean carrots.

"Go a oonu bed, yuh have to wake up early a mawning to follow me to catch the truck," she'd say once we were done.

In the early-morning I would be awakened by the rumbles of her gathering her goods and waking my siblings. It was cold in the morning, cold enough the fog overshadowed the whole place. Mother and all those who were going with her to meet the market truck had to grab sweaters. Those who had no sweaters had to put on extra clothes. Where we lived at night the temperature would be far below 50 degrees. So, it's not surprising those early 4 A.M. mornings were so cold. Mother never wanted me out in the early morning dew. My older siblings, mostly my brothers, were the ones going to help her load the farm goods on the market truck with fully stocked baskets or sewn plastic bags firmly balanced on their heads as makeshift "cata."

For sure, if mother didn't cook on market days, there was such an abundance of crops on our land I made it my duty to eat what I wanted. When it was possible my siblings would roast up some potatoes and green bananas. Dare someone pay no attention to the fire and burn up those. It would be such a tragedy. We wasted nothing. The knives came in handy because all that burnt crisp was going to be scraped off until it was good enough to eat. A few times when mother was off to the market, Dada stepped in and made us dinner. His dinner was his favorite "run down," a one-pot meal that consisted of every ground food mixed in coconut milk.

I never learned how to make it. Even if I did, it wouldn't come close to how he made it taste. That man cooked that meal as if he was preparing a grand feast, and he served it to us with pride. Even though the serving was just enough to fill up your corner teeth, we loved it and at times wished mother would go to the market more so we could get it. That was never the case though. It was not every day that the crops were at their best for reaping. Some days there was nothing for the market but just enough to feed the family and share with the neighbor.

Not only was mother a farmer and a cook for us, she was also the community seamstress and baker. She would sit around her little Singer sewing machine and make uniforms for just about every student going to the local schools. She even made dresses for my sisters and I using spare curtains. She was skilled with the craft of designing wedding cakes and traditional Christmas cakes. I would watch her in the kitchen as she mixed all the ingredients and carefully decorated those cakes. She was particular with her craft, especially the designs. She never went to school to learn those skills. As a matter of fact, she never made it past the fourth grade. It was just a God given gift and talent, and I never met anyone else like that. This woman was exceptional and unforgettable.

Mother would place those beautifully decorated cakes on the little dining table and smile as she looked at them admiring their beauty. She'd tell us not to even look at them much less touch them. Believe me, it was very tempting to put a finger on the edge of one of those cakes. Chances are if one of us did, a wooden spoon, most likely the same wooden spoon she used to mix the ingredients, would reach our hands, and fix our business. Come time to deliver the cakes, she would drape them in her best sheer covering and carefully hand them over to whoever was assigned to pick up cake.

As young as I was, even I understood she meant business with the directions she gave to the person carrying those cakes. Now, she did not only make wedding cakes, but she was also known for her traditional rum cake or black cake too. They made Christmas the most exciting and best times at home. I spent all year waiting for Christmas day knowing the treat I would receive. When mother gathered her ingredients for the cake and poured everything in the baking pan on the wooden fireplace, those cakes would come out perfect. That was the awesome part, but the best part was when she called "Stee," and I ran to the kitchen to get the wooden baking spoon to lick off all the mixture while she would give the mixing bowls to the others to share.

The taste of nutmeg, vanilla, sugar, butter, flour, eggs, and that last drop of her love would sweep on my tongue as I savored every bit. Most people called that cake "rum cake," but there was no rum or any form of liquor in her mixture. Mother's strong Christian belief forbade her from liquor. So, she made those cakes with excellence, liquor free. I believe after everyone ate it, they forgot it was called the world famous Jamaican black cake without the overproof rum or wine. After all that licking out of the cake pan and spoon, then there came the extra treat from my father on Christmas day. We never drank soda, but this day was the one time of the year that was an exception. Mmm the taste of soda on my tongue. My father would go to town and purchase a whole crate of soda. First, he would ask all his children what flavor they wanted, and then he would get just that. Such a smart way to avoid confusion.

This was also the time where more family members would visit, so they would get the leftover soda after my siblings and I got ours. Sometimes we'd taste a little and hide the bottle away from each other or the extra family members. After we received a nice slice of the delicious cake or potato pudding mother made, in the bright sunshine and our clean clothes we'd line up in the front yard as he called us one by one. With a smile plastered over my face, I took my bottle of pineapple soda.

He'd say, "Merry Christmas Stacy."

"Merry Christmas, Dada," I'd respond as I walked away to sit waiting for my siblings to join me with theirs.

It was funny. Even though we all wanted a specific flavor, after everyone got their soda, we went on a tasting rampage.

"Mek me taste yours," we'd say as we all took turns tasting each other's flavor.

That was the best day ever, no partiality or criticism amongst us. We all had our choice of soda and the same size slice of cake.

Christmas gifts were minimal. They consisted of a pair of socks or a new undergarment. When I was about nine or ten, mother went to town and bought a pretty red dress with little flowers on it with matching ribbons for my hair. This was to attend the yearly Christmas service at church. It was no question that I was cute in my dress. It was probably the best one she could afford, and it fit me nicely. Traditionally, the Sunday School children had to perform their little skits or sing the song they practiced all year. Was I up front in my pretty dress? Nope, I always ended up in the back row because of my height. I'd hoped maybe they would give me a chance in the front just once.

Do you know who was in the front? The ones who had the lead part. Can I tell you, one of my sisters always got the lead. Wouldn't bother to mention which one, but she was extra with the mic too. When she opened her mouth, you could hear her a mile or more away. I did finally get my chance to be upfront on the mic, but it wasn't Christmas time. It was during Rally, which was another one of those events where the children had to perform. However, this time after we sang, our parents had to pay for us to sit down. It was my moment, and I sang. Then I waited for my dad to pay for my seat. What was crazy is if you did not have your parents there, you would have been the last child standing. Dada never left us feeling as if we had nobody. So, no matter where he was, he would show up and pay for my siblings and I. My hero! I told you he never let us feel or experience dire deficits.

Another natural sweetness of Christmas was the fresh pine tree that was cut and carried by my brothers every year. We would make handmade decorations with old newspaper, greeting cards from "foreign," or other paper, strung all over the tree with the few Christmas lights we had. Sometimes half of them were not working because they were the same lights from year to year. However, when that tree lit up it was so exciting, and the excitement would increase if those lights had music in them. There was so much laughter and fun in our tiny living room as we told stories and sat close to the tree. The house would be freshly painted, and pretty sheets would be on our beds, possibly only for the day then nighttime back to the old sheets.

The season of Christmas was just special. You would think the Queen was visiting with the extra preparations that took place. Then after December 31st, we went back to normal. During this time, I used to make up stories and add to the famous "Anansi" storyline. I never wanted the feeling of Christmas to end. With all the extra excitement and food for that one day, I had such a deep feeling of appreciation and celebration and never wanted it to end. You would have the intention and love from everyone's heart, not just my family, but the entire community. Things like this are what give me the sweet reflections of my country life in Jamaica. Besides the cake, soda, and all the little fun and games that time of the year also some losses.

I watched how community men, including my dad, would kill pigs and goats in my backyard. My father would distribute or rather sell to the neighbors who were lacking meat for the holiday. That added so much to the festivities as I looked at their faces filled with joy. Families didn't have to go to town to buy meat for the holiday. Not everyone had livestock. So, just getting the opportunity to get or purchase fresh meat was an act of kindness and extra blessings for everyone. Those were moments that showed me how to invest first in a community, my community.

I believe my mother's gift of sharing was her ultimate calling. She would not only give from her pot, but from her heart as well, and it radiated through her smile. Each time she stretched her hands or extended her heart, her smile would widen, and you would see that twinkle in her eyes. Every plate she served to her own children, as well as the visiting neighbors and family, was filled with love. Her compassionate heart was clear to everyone. As I look back at my childhood memories with a humble and grateful heart, I would have to name my parents the power couple of all time, for all they did for everyone and most of all for the glory of God.

CHAPTER 4

Community Love

The tiny living room was arm wide and had a little black and white TV. I often imagined what those TV characters would look like in color. The creative idea to put yellow plastic wrap over the TV was brilliantly done by one of my siblings. Oh, so smart, now everyone on the TV looked alike. With that one TV, neighboring children would come to be a part of the living room audience for the famous television program, "Ring Ding," before going to their homes. The day came when we got the lovely gift of a color television. Hooray! My family was the first to get a color television in the community. The news spread and suddenly the house flooded with almost everyone from the community to sit and watch all the programs in color. Who said we were poor? If that is what poor looks like, then I need a new definition. We were blessed among the community as a family, and our name today still resounds with the utmost respect.

Going to church was not an option in my parents' home. I was always excited to go to the house of God. Mother was faithful in serving in the church and even more faithful to involve her children as well. Late on Saturday evenings we would start our preparation for church on Sunday: shine your shoes, clean your socks, iron your clothing, and get your hair done. I did less because mostly everything was done by my older siblings. I would just sit aside and suck my fingers, daydreaming about traveling in the sky.

See, I grew up in what some call the "black church," but I call it Pentecostal, Holy Ghost filled, water baptized church, with music to fill your soul for years to come, where pastors preached, and you would be saved at the sound of their voices. I remember this one time where the preacher gave a sermon on hell and suddenly shut off the lights.

He said, "Tomorrow is not a promise."

I'm not sure how many times I got saved, but I made it into tomorrow after all, not just one tomorrow, but many. I really want to thank God for keeping me, he is so faithful.

On Sundays I would be the first to get ready. I sat in my pretty frilly socks and shoes with an old tee shirt over my dress just to eat breakfast. The sound of gospel music such as Mahalia Jackson, The Five Blind Boys of Alabama and so forth played in the background. Mother would never let us leave the house without eating. She never wanted her children to look at someone else's food, ask for food, or look hungry. After breakfast, she would pack my little purse with a couple of dry crackers and butter and my little offering, which normally was $0.25 or less. I gave my offering faithfully every Sunday hoping that she would buy me an extra snack like an ice pop from the little shop at the corner of the church building.

Sometimes the ice pop or fudge stick man, Fudgy, would ride his bike selling ice pops by the church gate. He knew what time to come around, and all the little children would run outside at the sound of his distinct honking. Not getting an ice pop was the saddest thing on Sundays. My father, who went to another church, would sometimes catch Fudgy on his way back down and if I was lucky, he would buy me one. Hmm, I can still taste the flavor of that fudge melting in my mouth as I think back to those sunny Sunday afternoons. Money was not there for all my siblings to get a fudge stick, so I had to sometimes share mine with my sister.

In the Pentecostal church, your participation was a must whether you liked it or not. Whether you were in the choir, played an instrument, played the tambourine, collected offering, or gave your testimony when it was time for testimonies you were required to participate. If not, the older ladies would give you that look and pinch you if you dared to fall asleep during service. Certain times of the year would be special church services that rolled into the late hours of the night called convention or rally.

Convention services were the nights when everybody would get saved. After the preacher preached, he stood on the platform and surveyed the congregation.

He said, "Is there anyone who wants to accept Lord Jesus Christ as your personal savior?"

No one would answer. He would stay there for a while and make the plea again until maybe one person stood up and the usher escorted them to the front. Maybe a few would get up, but all the young children especially my age group would hide under the wooden benches.

"Me nah go up deh," we mumbled.

God forbid one of us would get up to go up to the altar, chatters would fill up under the benches again.

"Jesum piece, yuh a go," we'd say to each other.

Well after my friend got up, I became scared, but I followed behind her anyway unaware of what the outcome would be.

I used to see all those people running around the church, screaming, and shouting, speaking in different languages, and then some would fall out on the floor. To fall out always seemed like you caught the Holy Spirit, but I was not sure if I wanted the Holy Spirit. Once you reached the front of the church to accept Jesus, an older person would come and whisper, "You want to be saved?" After you replied yes, they would pray with you. One of those Convention nights I got saved. When I went to school the next day something transpired, and someone told me I had turned back. Well, it was going to be another service Monday night, so I would get saved again.

We were allowed to be in service despite the fact it was a school night. No one asked any questions or showed any concern that it was a school night. We had to be there. If mother was going, we all were going, and she was definitely going because she had a lot of responsibilities. I participated in everything for the Sunday School departments. Even though I had a shy demeanor and spent most of the time in the back during participation, it was never an option not to partake. Everything Pentecostal was a must from ladies not wearing pants or perming their hair, to just being saved.

As a little girl I often liked to wander off by myself in quiet places. There I would talk to myself as if there was company with me. My conversations were very quiet almost from within me. My favorite spot was under a tree or in the closet. During those times I would feel so peaceful and safe, not that there was danger around. It was just a different feeling than being in the company of my family. Unaware, this was the beginning of how God was preparing me to go into the secret place and listen to him for myself. It was his way to separate me from the crowds and distractions of the world around me. Although I was not clear on what was taking place, somewhere in the back of mind there was a belief that one day the true revelation would come forward.

It's obvious there has been a calling on my life ever since those moments as a child, and I'm grateful for the preparation. No one taught or assured me of the knowledge of what the calling of God meant. We were only taught to have reverence for the Elders in the church and of course for God. So, when I discovered the calling of God for my life, it ignited my spirit to such a great extent. I can look back to all the lessons I learned in my younger years; and now as a mother of four, instill as much as possible in them. One thing I continuously enforce is self-reliance, for that helped me to learn many valuable lessons.

Growing up my older brother Lennox, nicknamed "Alrie" and who is now an anointed Pastor in Jamaica, was always one of my favorite brothers. He would carry me on his back as we'd go back and forth to church up those rocky tiny roads, especially at night when it was dark. There weren't any streetlights, so we had to rely on the lights from neighboring houses which were distanced apart. When no light radiated from the neighboring houses, we'd be lucky to have someone with a small battery-operated flashlight. When the sound of a car approached, my brother would look to see if he recognized the driver. If he did, he would wave them down.

"Beg you a ride nuh," he said.

If he got a ride, of course he would take me with him while others continued to walk in the dark. When we got out of the vehicle, he would put me back up on his back and we'd continue up the hillside.

He loved to prank people. He would sneak in a bush with me still on his back and scare my other siblings or others as they passed by in the dark. His schemes would have me laughing while everyone else screamed. I really enjoyed those times with him. He would pretend he was a horse, while I bounced up and down on his back.

"Giddy up, giddy up," I'd say as I laughed even more.

All of those fun times made me feel so special, especially when I looked at the rest walking alongside him or in front breathing heavy out of tiredness. When he got married and moved away, I became extremely sad and missed all those special rides on his back.

He had married a beautiful lady and she suggested I come spend time with them in their new house. I looked forward to going there. They treated me as if I were their child. His wife had a younger sister with whom I later became friends, and she would come over for us to play together. As I became grown, moved away, then migrated to the US, they started their own family; H however, that did not stop or interrupt my relationship with them. To this day we still reminisce on those times and it brings me so much joy.

Alrie told me a story about myself that I barely recall.

He said, "Nobody was at home except the both of us. You were playing in the living room when you held onto the back of the chair. Suddenly both you and the chair fell to the floor and you hit your back. At that moment, you went speechless, had no pulse, and you became cold without any sort of movement. I scooped you up in my arms and spoke to God in my heavenly language. Suddenly you came back to life. That was when I first experienced a miracle happening right in front of me."

This once again showed me that God's plan for one's life is secured from an early age. It is assured he will prepare you through different situations and circumstances.

To God be the glory! My brother, Pastor Lennox Willis, is now walking in his healing ministry. Many have been healed from all kinds of infirmities and many who were demons got delivered and set free. He remained in his assignment understanding that some things were solely in God's hands.

CHAPTER 5

Foreign

$\mathscr{F}$oreign was that place everyone wanted to go. It was the United States of America, but my family was not on that list. Many days "foreigners" would come and visit the neighbors, or the neighbors traveled back and forth to see foreigners. However, the Willis family would only watch them and collect a small gift from the kindhearted receivers or travelers. It was not that we did not have family members living in foreign, they were just not coming that often like everyone else.

When the neighbors were not traveling or getting visitors, big barrels would be shipped to the prospective homes. You should've heard and seen the excitement on their faces. The excitement would start as soon as someone recognized the barrel on trucks that would transport it to these houses. Once the family receiving the barrel was revealed, the response from the community was heightened. What I knew for sure was once that barrel hit the prospective home, there would be local children going to that house hoping to get a small gift from foreign. Oftentimes the family would hand out a soap or maybe a toothpaste to another family. One of the soaps that came in the barrels was the good ole green Irish Spring. That was the best foreign soap, while we had our Jamaica favorite "carbolic" in our households.

We were one of the blessed families to receive something from those barrels. A few of my siblings' godparents would often receive a barrel. Although all of us weren't their godchildren, they cherished us just the same. So once that barrel was opened, they would shout from down the road for my mother to send one of us to collect our foreign tokens. Going to collect these goodies was extremely impressive. We would wash up, put on our clean clothes, vaseline or oil down our skin and hair, and off to the godparent's house we'd go.

One of the great things about that household was the family setting. We were like family to them, and I believe this was the only house we were allowed to eat from besides ours. When we went to collect our foreign goods, they would have us in one of their various rooms as they brought out the different items to take back to our house. What was amazing about this family was they would have two or more barrels at a time. So, going there was like going to the foreign store. One barrel would contain just food and the other would contain clothes. Yes, nice foreign clothes.

Even though we did not see when they originally opened the barrels, we knew big bags of Carolina rice and a big jug of vegetable oil were there. The godparents would open their bag of rice and distribute it in a small bag for us to take home. We'd go back home swinging plastic supermarket bags, which we called "scandal bags" in Jamaica, filled with our small portion of foreign goods. Sometimes the food we received from foreign was available in Jamaica, but we could not afford it. We were so grateful for our foreign goods, and mother would take her time using them, especially the soap. Mother would store the soap in the container she kept her clothes, and it would have her room spelling so sweet.

After receiving all those foreign things, I dreamed about going on planes many days and nights. I would see myself in those dreams flying across the sky going back and forth. Then I'd wake up sweaty with my heart pumping extremely hard only to realize it was just a dream. But it was a dream that was somehow waiting to happen. Those days of watching big pretty houses in the community with the hopes of going inside just to get a glimpse would wreck my mind. I was curious about how they lived. It wasn't that I did not like my house, I loved my house and family. There was just something special in the atmosphere, especially when they received foreign goods. Those goods would be stained with the scent of green Irish Spring soap, and you would know they had received a barrel, even if you did not see the transportation that dropped it off.

I remember the day when we finally got a barrel. It was a huge one from England. Most of the items in there were thick clothing, fancy shoes, and pretty thick curtains. Later, I learned a portion of my aunts, uncles, and cousins were living in England which explained all those winter items. It was clear they did not know us individually. However, they had to have some form of communication with my parents because the bottom of those shoes would have our names on them. Again, there were a lot of us, and they wanted to make sure none of us were left out from receiving. As mother pulled out all the things from the barrel, I could smell that foreign scent, each time she lifted her hands. We all would gather close enough to see what we got.

The interesting part was there was a pair of patent leather black shoes with "Stacey" taped to their bottom. They were really cute. My face lit up at the sight of them, and I could not wait to wear them. The thought of having them on my feet warmed my heart. Even if there was nothing else for me, I was satisfied with my pretty shoes. I would wear them to church and hope everyone would notice them and know they came from foreign. My feet slid into the shoes, but to my disappointment they were too big. My jaw dropped. I pushed my fingers in my mouth and mumbled while I took the shoes back to mother.

"Bow, my shoes too big," I said.

Mother had a way to fix everything.

She shoved up her mouth, "Yuh will grow inna it."

Right as she finished that sentence, I heard my name again. This time it was for a sweater. Indeed St. Andrew was cold, but not to the extent of those sweaters. They were the thick knitted ones that you needed during freezing weather. When the distribution was over, we would snuggle in whatever it was we received and was grateful that we finally got a barrel. As for my shoes that were too big, when it was time to wear them, mother stuffed it with an extra sock and some cotton from the cotton tree.

"You soon grow in it," she said as I tried to walk properly in them for church.

In no time the rocky roads had battered the bottom of those shoes, and soon I would have to take them to the shoemaker.

We would have to take such good care of those items not knowing when we would get another barrel. As I shared before, most of my clothes were hand-me-downs from my sisters. So, I was excited when I received a brand-new sweater or a frilly dress with my name on it. Mother was ready to tuck in and pull out her sewing machine as needed to adjust whatever clothes needed adjusting. I learned how to be content in whatever state I was in and to be grateful for everything in life which taught me so much humility.

CHAPTER 6

Unforeseen Dangers

My relationship with God was important to me.

A close friend said, "Stacy, you always go up to the front of the church and stare in amazement as the preacher preaches the word of God."

As I recall, the preaching was so powerful I would just cry, but I didn't know why. Every time there was an altar call, I would run up and squeeze in between people to stand right up front. I believe this was a part of the process to my destiny. Walking miles and miles without complaining was normal when it was time to go to church, healthcare, or school. Running up and down the hill, sometimes I had to walk through gullies to get to my destination. I would fall because of an unaware force or the excess amount of rocks that pierced my feet which caused me to fall flat either on my butt or my knees. With bumps and bruises I would cry or sometimes laugh it off and get up to finish my journey for it all played a part in my process.

Many times, the wayward community children would hide themselves in bushes and throw stones or other objects. I got injured on several occasions. My brother would go searching to see who the culprits were, but they would run away leaving me to suck it up and carry on. However, once I found out who the troublesome children were, I would inform my mother and without a doubt she would address the parents in a calm manner. I always tried to avoid conflict. Maybe it was because of my shy demeanor.

There was one time when one of the boys in my class hit me. I wanted to hit him back but was intimidated by his size. After school dismissed, I started to walk home with my sister and brother. I told my sister that the boy hit me in class. She ran up to the boy who was walking in front of us with his friends.

"A which one a oonu lick my sista," she said.

No response. I was scared as I watched my sister question the group of boys again.

Yelling back at me, "Which one a dem hit you?"

I barely opened my mouth, "Juba Broadhead!"

I had no idea what my sister was about to do so I stood next to my brother as I watched her.

She yelled, "Come lick him back!"

As the boys tried to walk away, she barred them.

"Oonu nah go no weh."

In such a frightened state, I barely stepped up to the boy and slapped him on his hand, but the boy did not shake as if he did not feel the hit.

"That a no nothing, lick him again," she said.

My body trembled as I attempted to hit him again, but this time my sister grabbed my hands, doubled up my fist, and knocked the boy right in his big head. I felt every bone in my fingers crack and thought a couple of my fingers were broken. Thank God they didn't because I don't know what story I would've had for mother when I got home that evening.

"A bet yuh nuh touch my sister again," my sister warned him.

She was such a warrior with her feisty ways.

My family was always close knit. No one or nothing could have ever come between us. I cannot remember much conflict with my siblings except for dinner time when one of my brothers would trick me into looking away so they could steal some of my food. As skinny as I was, having less food on my plate was not cool at all; but that still did not result in a conflict. I would just finish eating what I had left and then suck my fingers, and mother would slap my brother for taking my food. One thing for sure --, none of us had more food than the other because mother had a way of serving us, and we were happy with the amount of food we got.

Now, if the truth be told, I was an inquisitive little girl that loved to wander off in strange places. One time my wandering and curiosity exposed me to unforeseen danger. I was about nine years old, and I told my mom that I was going to our neighbor's house to play with my friend. This was the only friend's yard I was allowed to go to freely. Her mother and my mother were so close. They even had a special sound when they called each other from their yards. So, it was okay to go visit that specific family. Although the community itself was close knit, we were not allowed to just show up at anyone's house. As a matter of fact, the distance to walk to the other neighbors' houses was further than this one family. There were many turns and corners. I knew my parents, especially my mother, did not want me on the road by myself.

Going to a neighbor's house would be under a couple of conditions. Mother would have to send us there, and she would time us going and coming back. She warned us not to go there and stare at their pots or eat from anyone. Since all the houses were visible yet far, she would stand in the front or back of the house and watch us go to these neighbors' houses. Then we had to wave to her saying we got there safe. If the time to return home had passed, she would start calling our names and nothing could stop the speed we would pick up to get back home. Yes, we had to get back before it got dark. So, there would be no days she would send us anywhere close to the setting of the sun. Mother was one wise woman and very sensitive in her spirit.

This particular day when I told my mother I wanted to go play with my friend, she stood in the yard and called to my friend's mother to let her know I was on my way there. "Sen har come," my friend's mother responded.

Mother turned to me, "Gwaan Stacy."

I skipped down the rocky path with my pale skin displayed from my little blouse and shorts. Mother stood there and watched me cross the small street that separated our gate and the neighbor's then the mothers waved to each other that I was safe. My mother could overlook the neighbor's yard and watch me. I used to say mother had eagle eyes. The moment I was not in the front of the neighbor's house where she could see me, she would walk down the path towards their house. And when she got closer and did not hear me playing, she would call my name. Now we were not allowed to go in the houses of these neighbors even if mother sent us there. So, if we're not in the backyard we had better be in the front of that house where an adult could see us.

I was at my friend's house, and although I have no recollection as to why my curious mind allowed me to wander away, I ended up in another neighbor's house. There he was a man about 30 years older than I was living with his wife and two sons. I'm not sure of the tactic he used to lure me inside his house, but it worked. All I could recall was standing outside his door knowing we were not allowed to go in anyone's house. I remember hearing the smoothness of his voice as he started to sing a well-known gospel song. It was that special song we learned early on to invite Jesus Christ in our lives. The words were, "Come into my heart. Come into my heart Lord Jesus. Come in to stay, come I pray, come into my heart Lord Jesus."

His voice echoed to me. The sound of that song melted my heart and touched my spirit. My insides became warm as he kept singing to me as if it was a lullaby. He must have taken my hand and led me inside because the quietness of the room had now become just a space for only the two of us. He motioned for me to lay on top of his crotch. It felt good resting on his grown crotch, and why would it not feel good? The soothing song had dismissed any other thoughts out of my head. So there was no reason why laying there would not feel good. I loved that song, and at that time I did not see anything wrong with laying on him just to listen to that song. It felt like I was "getting saved" at church. The only difference was it was not church, and I was in close proximity to a grown man touching his manhood with my tender nine-year old self.

Where was his respect for me, his family, my family, the community, or himself? What was his intention for a fragile soul as I? As I laid there on top of him, my head rested halfway or less on his body. As he started to hum in my ears, I could feel his hand trying to manipulate towards my side, but it was at that moment I heard the spirit of my mother's voice.

"Stacy, where are you?"

It seemed as if I snapped out of unconsciousness and immediately raised up my trembling body as the voice of my mother's spirit got louder in my ears. I ran out of his house, hurried past my friend as she came out of her kitchen with her dinner bowl in her hand, and then ran past her father who was in the front of the yard.

I became breathless as I sped through their broken gate, across the little streets and up the hill to my house without saying a word to anyone. Believe me when I tell you that my mother was standing in the front of the yard with her hands on her hips.

She asked, "But a wah happen Stacy?"

She must have seen the frightened look on my face, but I didn't understand what happened so I could not answer her. It was almost sundown and knowing I needed to be in the house before seemed as if I was about to be disciplined. Turns out the neighbors thought I went home when they did not notice me playing with my friend or heard my voice. However, the fact that I did not tell them bye was a solid curious moment for me that almost turned tragic.

Standing in front of my mother, I felt safe and shameful at the same time. Her puzzled face settled as she continued to look at me.

"You better go for your dinner," she said as she sucked her teeth.

Everyone was already around the table having their dinner. By the time I pulled up my train next to my brother, he was almost done with his food.

He leaned over to me, "Stacy a which part you did deh?"

I refused to answer just the same way I refused to answer my mother. After I came to my full senses later that night and had to lay next to my brother for our regular bedtime sleep pattern, I knew what that man tried to do to me was disgusting and dirty. He laid there with a perverted sinful state of mind to satisfy his sexual desires using me as a tool. And we all know sin feels good, but only for a while.

The effect of such an incident would have torn my innocence into pieces far beyond my flesh. But God. I can still see the bearded face of this grown man, and his breath still tickles my nose. The dim room remains as a shadow in my memory, a shadow of disbelief and disappointment as the community I love so much almost became a "talk about incident" that probably would have caused division in every section. I kept the thought of what that man would have done to me in the darkest section of my being. If my mother's spirit did not call me, what would have been the result? What would have happened if I had told my brothers or my father? There was no doubt the outcome of this grown man living with his family would've been tragic.

I learned from that day not to go wandering away, especially in someone else's home. So anywhere my mother went I was holding on to her skirt tail or walking in the shadow of my older siblings for protection. Every time I would bump into that man, I would cringe and look at him with a scared face. I never went back to my friend's yard unless I was going there with my mother.

CHAPTER 7

The Hurricane

The rain vigorously hit against the zinc roof. I watched the ceiling leak as the pounding wind and rain pranced across the few glass windows we had. The water ran off the roof into the blue drum containers at the side of the house. We heard the news of a hurricane expected to land on the Island. It was hurricane season and Jamaica was anticipating the dreadful beating from Hurricane Gilbert. In a flash, it could hit the island in full force. The evening got dark quickly, and my father and brothers tied the goats and pigs up under the cellar.

We all sat around our little TV as we watched the weather report. Suddenly the wind whispered on the outside as it brushed up against the banana trees. Then it got louder "whoosh" and louder, "whoosh, whoosh" as it howled across the field.

"Plug out the TV," mother shouted from behind us.

The sound of big raindrops bounced on the window in front of us. We stared at the shadowy images of the tree leaves while they formed funny images. Some looked like dancing men, others looked so scary we were sure it was duppy. Whenever those shapes scared me, I came up with ways to create funny stories to match them.

"Tat, tat," the water drops hit the table in front of my mother as she sat there watching dada eat his meal. Each one of us fumbled for a container to catch the water. It didn't matter whether it was a bucket, pail, basin, cup, or dish; just anything to avoid the floor, bed, or table getting soaked. Those rainy nights at home were the worst and at times were the best. The good thing is all that rain would fill up the different sizes of containers at the corner of the house with water. Having those containers filled meant we did not have to go fetch water at the standpipe a mile or two away. However, it would make the house colder where we would sleep in sweaters or extra sheets because we had no warm blankets.

The most tragic thing ever was that night the hurricane hit the Island with force. We had done our regular bedtime routine of telling duppy stories before going to sleep. Later I was awakened by the sound of the wind hollering over the roof and the squeaking of the loose door in my room. The force of the wind was more than usual, and the rain banged right along with it. Suddenly, the speed of the breeze increased with such great force as it whistled or maybe screamed above my head. I guess you'd call that the "hurricane breeze."

The sound became louder but now it had a splashing sound with it. I fully woke up and felt extra cold as if we had no covering on the bed.

"Gawd, why it so cold?" I said to myself.

The cold air stung my skinny frame as I pulled the thin floral sheet over my head. But the sheet felt moist. I knew I had not peed the bed, so why was the sheet moist? The rain and the wind clashed in harmony against the house and created a musical sound. As I lifted my head in the dark, there it was, the dark starry sky piercing down at me from a corner of the ceiling. I thought maybe I was dreaming, and I would wake up and tell no one about this dream. I rubbed my eyes and looked over at my brothers who were sound asleep. No, it was not a normal rainy night.

Raindrops squeezed through the tiny holes in the ceiling and made them seem bigger than usual. As I looked over at my brothers in their beds, unaware of the extra leaks over my bed, I pulled myself up and tried to call them in a quiet tone, but no response. I wanted to call them a little louder but didn't want to wake up the entire household. I called them again as I sat up in the bed hoping at least one of them would wake up; and again, they continued their slumber. Just then I heard the squeaky sound of my parent's room door opening and the dragging sound of my mother's slippers across the tile floor. The sound enveloped my heart as a sign of help as she approached my room. She flicked the light on and noticed a section of the floor was already wet.

She called, "Stacy! Stacy! Get up and come!"

Guess she figured the boys would wake themselves from the panic in her voice as it echoed in the small room, but that was not the case. She dragged the sheet off them and called them out of their sleep.

"But wait a minute oonu don't hear what is happening outside. My gawd but a what smatta," she said.

There is something about that midnight cry. This time around no containers were going to help with the leaks. It was not those ordinary rainy nights. It was a vicious hurricane. There were leaks in all corners of the room and our things started to dampen. My brothers rushed out of the bed while I went in the corner of the tiny living room and sucked my fingers. As I looked up at the ceiling, the force of the wind lifted it up inch by inch. The zinc roof started to bang against the wind as if they were playing musical chairs. I paused to listen as the rain angrily beat against the house. At one point I felt as if the solid brick house shook out of place.

I had never experienced a hurricane before, and I would not like to experience nothing like it again. The uncertainty of what would result from the hurricane was somewhere in my subconscious as I tried to stay focused. Within minutes there was no place for shelter. The ceiling was being ripped off faster than I could blink my eyes. With my heavy eyelids I watched my brothers and dad hurry through the house constructing different plans to keep us safe. But there was no way for them to manage the dashing winds and rain. Every brick and sandbag that dad had put on the roof in preparation for the hurricane had now shifted or blown off from the force of the wind. He concluded the best thing to do was find a corner of the house and stay there with hope of survival.

Dada was not going outside, but outside came to him when the front door blew right off. Danger had now made its way in the house. The debris, flowers, and everything else that was in the yard made its way in the house. The door broke off and almost landed on the very table we sat earlier for our dinner. My screams and cries were so loud with the hope I would not die in this dreadful storm. My fingers were not going to comfort me this time around. No one warned or prepared me for this kind of catastrophe. Only if all the time I spent going to church they had told me that during a storm I should pray and watch God; then maybe my worried soul would not have been in despair as I watched my house crumble with my family and I inside.

Water rushed through the house from the ceiling and the broken door at such a speed accompanied by lightning and wind. It was so scary. We moved and now had to make decisions in darkness as mother had unplugged the lamps, TV, and radio. There was no doubt my mother's quiet spirit was praying because she said very little as she tried to keep me warm with an extra sheet from her room. One of my brothers snuggled under the sheet with me as if we were two frightened cats. You could hear the wailing as the community struggled in the midnight hour while hurricane Gilbert battered their farms, and houses. Every voice echoed with despair and tormented my spirit because I never heard anything like that before.

Lights flickered, electric wires gnashed throughout the fields, and then the whole place went dark as the power went out. My heart pounded against my tiny chest at the sudden darkness. There was nothing funny about it, and no time for duppy stories or any other stories. Mother struggled through the dark towards the dining room and to light the kerosene oil lamp on the table. She had two of them, and they were tiny enough to fit in any corner. The ray of light from the lamp gave us hope as the storm raged on. Mother held it up and looked at her frightened children cuddled up on the two-seat sofa and came over to us.

She said, "Come, go under the bed," as she hurried and pushed me under the bed in my older brother's room.

For some reason I always felt safe and warm in that room, as if it was a secret anointing in there. The deep red polish on the wooden floor welcomed me, and I did not care if I would be colored red after that. The floor was freshly polished a couple days back and at that time I was mad with my brothers for stepping on it after I spent time on my knees polishing it. You see, the time I spent on my knees cleaning those floors taught me how to stay on my knees with GOD in prayer.

My father realized his attempts to save the house were

no longer in his hands. He sent his boys under the bed next to me and warned us not to come out until the storm was over. My parent's room was across from us, and I watched as their feet stepped out of sight into their section of the house. I had no doubt that they went into their room and made an agreement with God, asking him to save their family from this horrible hurricane. My father knew the efforts he had put out to build that house. Every brick that went into building it was carried by his hand. He didn't have the money to pay for transportation because he needed the money for the mason worker. There was no doubt in my mind that he knew if God saved his family and gave him strength, he would be able to rebuild it. He was a determined, hardworking man that was full of resilience.

As I folded myself under the bed on the cold floor next to my brothers, my eyes became sleepy. I wondered if that was the end of my life. I wanted to survive and wanted my family to survive, but most of all I wanted to go "foreign." I also wondered if this was judgement day. The preachers always said Jesus would come like a thief in the night, and it was nighttime. Was Jesus coming? Was I saved? Would I go to Heaven or hell?

I asked one of my brothers, "Do you think it is judgement day?"

He started crying, "Me no know."

Something had to be done because I wanted to be saved again. So, I mumbled the Lord's prayer. I heard my brother mumbling something too as his voice trembled behind me. Minute by minute time drifted away from us in the cold dark room.

My brother whispered, "Stacy."

I did not answer as my body folded up like a turtle in its shell.

He called again, "Stacy, you sleeping?"

I refused to answer. My spirit finally drifted off to sleep as he hugged me tight. We remained under the bed in the moist cold sheet the whole night, sleeping as much as we could through the hollering sound of the hurricane. I thought that night would never end.

CHAPTER 8

The Recovery

*A*s my eyes opened the next morning, I was greeted by the sound of my mother's slippers on the wet floor coming towards the room. She gave a slight push on the somewhat shaky door.

"Stacy," she called in her soft and calming voice.

My only response was to crawl out from under the bed and stop at her feet as if I had no strength to get up. The house was a wreck. There were broken windows, fallen ceiling, broken doors, debris from outside, and water everywhere. All our clothes and books were soaked. Now what? How will I study or sleep in my bed?

The hurricane was over, but the sky still had dark clouds. I put on my slippers as we all surveyed the damage outside. The once flourishing farm and field that held our provisions was uprooted and the trees had fallen or blown away. Good thing, the bananas that I loved so much were now in my reach, but almost everything else was scattered. Mother walked to her favorite place, the kitchen, and it was dust, totally crumbled. The only thing that was left in place was the concrete fireplace with the dark shadow of where she prepared our meal the night before. The place looked clean and dirty at the same time. We had a lot of cleaning up to do from sweeping up the yard to mopping out the house. Everyone was hands on at work, and mother tried to figure how she would feed her family.

Pieces of wood that mother normally used for the fire were wet, even though my father had stored some in the house before the hurricane. Although my father's education was limited, he was a smart man. His innovative skills were nothing less than a person who went to a technical school. He used that innovation to prepare for the hurricane as best he could. For most of the day we ate fruits and had bread or hard excelsior (Jamaica brand) crackers with butter later. There was no drinking water available, only water to wash up with. Thank God for the containers on the house corner that were filled up and overflowed.

The clothes that were hand washed by mother earlier in the week now had to be put out to dry. Unfortunately, the clotheslines from all the sections of the yard had been ripped from the feeble poles. I was grateful for the remaining trees, flowers, and bushes because we used them for our clothes to be hung out and dried. As Mother and I stood in front of the house looking down at the neighbor closest to us, their house was in place.

Mother yelled to inform them, "We survived."

The neighbor replied, "We too! Thank God."

We walked a little further towards the neighbor as they shared their experience across the battered field. I wanted to visit my friend, but then I remembered that terrible grown man who tried to take advantage of my innocence. So, I stayed right next to my mother as I sucked my fingers and listened to their conversation.

Evening time slowly crept in on us. We did not have any hot meals; but mother, God bless her, fed us enough water and crackers as we wiped up instead of washed up. We gathered in the house around the kerosene lamp until it was nightfall, and we all went to sleep without complaining. I never learned to complain about much. As a matter of fact, what was there to complain about anyway?

Day two after the hurricane was a bit on the brighter side. The sun came piercing through the sky as if we did not just have a huge hurricane. As I looked across the island from the top of the mountain, the beauty of the place was such a renewed sight. Now that there was no kitchen, my brothers gathered up pieces of sticks and brushes that were scattered all over the yard. They chopped them up and put them in the spot where mother had her kitchen. I tell you; God has a sense of humor. He makes provision in different ways.

You should have seen mother's smile brighten as she

gathered the sticks they gave her and created a makeshift fireplace. She rinsed her pots, and she was ready. Mother poured that kerosene oil on those sticks and struck a match; but nothing, no fire. Her medium frame titled over that spot and blew onto it, one spark. She took a deep breath and blew again, more sparks. She grabbed a plate and fanned those sparks, then kaboom! There came the fire. That big metal pot went on and she meant business as she hummed while making our favorite, that good old cornmeal porridge.

Yellow cornmeal was often cooked in our house. They used to call it "tun cornmeal," but she knew how to make the "tun cornmeal" in fancy dishes. Mother was a creative cook. She would add red beans, pumpkin, or carrots in her cornmeal and serve it up with tin mackerel. Delicious wasn't even the word to describe how good it was. She would sweeten up that porridge with some condensed milk. When the milk seemed extra thick, she blew it out with her mouth from the two holes she made on the top of the can for it to run out. After the milk seemed just about finished, she took a knife and carved around the top and rinsed the can out leaving no waste. A refrigerator wasn't added to my household until a few years later, but it was cold enough on the mountain top of St. Andrew to preserve our food. Nothing went to waste.

Ants and flies often swarmed opened containers, so it was best to open the top and scoop out the milk, then get a wet towel and cover it on the table. Talking about cornmeal, she had a way of frying up some dumplings with extra cornmeal in it. She kneaded with butter and a little flour to hold it in place, but it was that yellow cornmeal porridge that made everything wonderful from that kitchen. Mother served my father his two slices of hard dough bread and butter. Then it was my turn.

"Stee," she called with a melody in her voice.

I skipped to her and there was my little plastic mug with my porridge in her hand. Inside were pieces of buttered bread where you could see the melted butter as it simmered on the top of my cup.

I balanced my cup in my hand with my spoon and went to sit in the doorway and watched her through the little wooden door of the kitchen as I ate my porridge right up. As I shooed away flies, chickens, and the two dogs from around me, the image of my mother sitting in the smoky kitchen while eating dumplings was the very sight of her sacrifice for her family. Just the thought of her not even coming out of the kitchen but making sure we all were served, showed how remarkable she was. It was not clear then why she never came out of the kitchen; but as I got older, I came to a solid conclusion that she was just ready to serve more food.

There were days where the community children would just show up and if feeding them meant she needed to ignite that fire again she was ready. When everyone had their porridge, the sound of scraping came echoing from the big pot as she scraped out the thick residues in the bottom. Mother would call my brothers and I to share all the extra scraps. To be honest, that was the best part of the porridge. It tasted extra sweet, and if it was sitting for a while, it became crunchy.

Despite the country being shut down at that time, including no electricity, life went on in the community during the day as normal as possible. At night it was a standstill, quieter and maybe by 5 P.M. it was bedtime. You bet I knew what 10 or more hours of sleep felt like because there was no wasting of kerosene for studying or playing around. The lamp was only essential if my father was not at home before sundown and he had to eat when he got home. Mother would use the dim lamp to put on the table in front of Dada as he ate his room temperature meal. There was no heating up of meals. Food was prepared early, and his serving was placed on the table fully covered under what they called a "dish cover," which was a plastic mesh cover used to prevent flies or any other bugs from getting in the food. Then mother would drape her nice dish towel over it and wait for her husband to come and feast on her scrumptious meal.

The tiredness of my father would often show when he ate. I remember watching him fall asleep around the table. Sometimes much of the food would still be on his plate as his head hung down over the food. You could hear the concern in my mother's voice as she sat across from him and called his name so he could finish eating. He'd then wash up and get to bed. Most of those times I would already be in bed, but from the dim light of the lamp I would get up and peep at my father sleeping around the table hoping he would finish his meal and go to sleep. I was not sure if I wanted to wake him or let him rest. Deep inside my heart I wanted him to rest. He worked so hard.

My father was not only a farmer, but he also worked diligently as a mechanic at the water commission for the entire district. While the community slept in the wee hours of the morning, he would be out there making sure everyone had nice clean flowing water when they got up. There were days I wouldn't see him until it was time for me to go to sleep or as he passed the school fence. When he walked past the school while I was in the school yard, I would dash to the fence and call out to him.

"Dada, Dada."

He would wave as he hurried pass, and with his strong voice he encouraged me.

"Go learn you lesson."

That usually made me feel so good seeing my father coming from work, and knowing he wanted me to get what he did not, which was to continue my education.

By the time lunch came with the sun in the middle of the sky scorching the dry ground, he was on the farm tilling his crops. When I got home from school he would still be somewhere on the farm. My father's presence was not a part of my life during the week. All that he was doing was for the love of his family, and I never lost my love and respect for him. I loved him even the more as I watched how hard he worked.

Every storm has its silver lining. I recall that after the rebuilding of the community, my house was not the same. We now had an inside kitchen, small bathroom, bigger

TV, and tile floors. Then there were those Fridays my father would go off to Kingston and bring us the best snacks they had on the market. We would wait down the road or by the door for him to come. He was discreet, and sometimes it would seem as if he brought nothing for us. I would wait for him to come in with his bag, but what he would do was place the plastic bags in his traveling bag as to trick us. I would just sit and stare at him while sucking my fingers hoping he had something from town for me. Occasionally, I would turn towards the TV and pretend I was not waiting for mine. When he was settled and had finished his dinner, he would call one of us to get his bag. Yes, the rush for that bag would have me sliding across the floor. My father was the best even though he tricked us sometimes. He taught us patience, and that was his way of playing with his children and making up for the days we did not spend time with him.

One of my favorite snacks was the good old fashioned animal crackers. I loved them then and I am still a fan of them now, even though my love of sweets is not the same. Whenever I want to remember those good old days, I search the stores for a bag of animal crackers and savor them just as if I was that little girl at my father's feet. That evening when he would distribute those crackers among his children, we would play with them as if we were putting on a show. We would break off the heads, tails, or feet, then see who eats their animal first. As a matter of fact, nobody wanted to eat theirs first due to the fear of not having any more crackers.

There were a lot of children to treat so no one child got a bag for themselves. We learned to share. So that was even more reason why no one wanted to eat all their crackers first. We also had the Shirley biscuits. We got really creative and playful with those. We gathered our pencils and traced every line on those biscuits. Our biscuits had black lines on them, but we ate them as if it were extra decorations. You could say we learned how to draw by tracing the design of those biscuits. It was not often, but there would be that extra special treat when we got Ovaltine biscuits instead. We went with the tracing on those biscuits too. Life was just fun and innocent in my house. Yet, we were still labeled as the "poorest family" in the community. Even still, our household served as a comfort zone, shelter, and entertainment for many besides us.

With my shoulders shrugged, a smirk on my face, and laughter in my heart I ask, "Could this really define us as the poorest family, or was it just the real meaning of my country life in East Rural St. Andrew, Jamaica?" The cock crowing at 5:30 A.M. indicating the break of the morning, drinking sugar water with a few of our meals, eating tun cornmeal, carrying water on our heads, sleeping in the same bed, and scrubbing the flooring; to me, were some of the fondest memories of the place where my parent's legacy started.

CHAPTER 9

The Great Migration

A few years went by and my sister, the one who held my fist to fight back that boy, moved away to Kingston. I became the only girl at home with my two brothers. It was somewhat fun, but I wanted my sister's company. I felt alone and lonely most of the time because I was not as rough as my brothers to climb trees or go to the fields. In those times, it was customary that the older siblings helped with the younger ones. But at the time my mother was not ready to let me leave from her. So, I stayed in the cold hills of St. Andrew until I was 13. Then mother decided to send me into Kingston to live with one of my older sisters and her family.

It was sort of nice because I had a baby niece to play

with along with her older brother. And boy oh boy was the temperature different from St. Andrew. It was so hot both day and night. The streets were busier, and things just looked strange. There were no fruit trees and no friends playing in their yards. I wasn't sure I wanted to stay there. I missed my parents, school, church, and fun with my friends. The only great thing was there were no more rocky roads, thank God.

When I tell you this Kingston living was totally different from my county life, I am so serious. Not only did that place have a different kind of hot, but they had a congregation of mosquitos always waiting for you. There was no freedom to run to a neighbor's house. Everyone was locked inside their own house, and you would have to go knock on their gates saying you needed to talk. I found that very strange. Mind you, the children in those houses, myself included, had to talk through the gates because no one was allowed inside.

On one of those extremely hot days while I was at home with my baby niece, I heard a banging on the gate in front of the house. It was my sister, yes that same sister who had taught me how to fight. At that time, she was living not too far away, and she got news that I was in Kingston and came to see me. If my memory serves me well, there was no phone call saying she was coming. I was so happy for the reunion. I even thought she was going to stay with me, and we would live together again. Unfortunately, it was not so, or at least not at that time.

As I was getting ready to be registered for school in

Kingston, I got news that I was going foreign. As a little girl my favorite television show was "The Cosby Show." I admired how well dressed, professional, and well-spoken Cliff Huxtable and his wife were. Their beautiful home was so impressive. Their family was not as big as mine, but they looked as if they had so much fun. There was no doubt they had lived in houses like the ones in Kingston because I never noticed them going to play outside. My imagination began to run wild as I thought of the day I would enter the United States of America, a land that flowed with milk and honey. Not sure who told me there was such a land.

The thought of milk and honey flowing was interesting, and I wondered if it would be free for everyone. I never had honey before but for sure I had milk; pure cow's milk squeezed from the cow. Although my parents were farmers, there were no cows on our farm. However, someone else in the community had one, and we would get fresh milk from them. Our community was very resourceful. Whatever one family didn't have access to, another would. We all learned to care and share with each other.

On June 16, 1990, my dreams became a reality. I was once again next to my mother and my "fighter" sister, as we headed to the Airport in Kingston to board a plane for the very first time. There I was with my thick jheri curls in my little brown short set, matching with my sister. As I faced my reality of flying in the sky, I wondered if I would see Bill Cosby when I got there. In those times going to foreign was the biggest highlight for any family, and for my family it seemed as if there was no chance of us leaving the mountaintop of St. Andrew.

I used to watch neighbors go back and forth from foreign or have visitors, but the Willis family was only on the farm. Going to the airport was bittersweet with family members crying from being left behind or missing those who were traveling. Traditionally it seems as if every family member would travel to the airport on the day of departure, but it would only be one or two people leaving, and the rest would turn and go back home. Well, on this hot summer day, I believe my family created history. Three members, myself, my sister, and my mother set foot on the plane to go to foreign.

We got to the airport early enough to give our final hugs before boarding. I stood in the hot sun as I looked at my beautiful baby niece in my sister's arms. As I hugged my sister and began walking away, my niece stretched her tender hands towards me.

She mumbled, "Mama, mama, mama."

I was not her mama, but from spending those precious moments with her she saw me as a mother figure. I was not sure if she could come with me. I wanted to take her, but she was not a part of the plan.

My eldest sister, Sleep-in-Peace Carlene, guided us through the process.

"Come on, oonu have to go check in now," Carlene said anxiously.

I did my final goodbyes and was elated walking

through the crowded airport. As we walked up to the counter my heart leaped as the representative questioned us. My sister answered all the questions. Our passports got stamped, and my sister made sure my mother's pocketbook was secured with all our important documents. We were set to board the plane.

"Have a safe trip," she said as she bid us goodbye.

The walkway to the plane was long. At one point I wondered how far we would have to walk for the plane. Butterflies filled my stomach at the thought of arriving in the U.S. I held my sister's hand as she walked in the middle with her arm tucked in mother's. To get to the plane we had to exit the building and walk out to the runway to board. There you would get the opportunity to see your family one last time as they stood across the other side of the airport screaming and waving. If you forgot what they were wearing, you could easily miss them with the large crowd bidding farewell to their families.

Mother took her first step up the stairs of the plane, and the wind blew her floral dress and lifted her nice summer hat off her head. I burst out laughing as I looked at my mother at the plane door trying to hold down her skirt and hat at the same time. She seemed nervous and never bothered to turn around to wave goodbye, even to her other children. It was my turn to go up the stairs and there was no looking back for me. I rushed up the stairs and heard a family member yell out my name from the other side of the airport. I turned, waved, and just like that I was gone away from them all. I realize now sometimes you must move forward in life and leave that what you know behind you. That's what we had to do on June 16, 1990.

My dad had traveled two months ahead of us. I was excited at the thought of seeing him when I got off the plane. The plane lifted and so did my spirit. I was finally soaring through the sky above the clouds that I dreamt about all those years. To be the "poorest family" from St. Andrew, it sure didn't feel like we were. We had five family members leave the island in the space of two months. God is faithful in all his promises.

"Welcome to JFK International Airport. Thank you for flying with us," the pilot said after the plane made a big bump on the ground.

Everyone cheered with praises as they thanked the airline crew. I was anxious to finally be in foreign. It was a tedious process in the airport now that my older sister was not present. She gave my fighter sister all the instructions on how she should handle things, as if she was familiar with the system. However, my eldest sister had never once traveled to America, but she seemed as if she were a frequent flyer with all the knowledge of what to do. She was so smart with a boss like demeanor. I loved her so much and miss her knowledge.

Here I was in a strange land with the hope to experience the land of milk and honey. I wondered why they depicted America in that way. Could it be an analogy of how smooth things would flow, or was it the highlight of different things there? We each had two suitcases. We had no idea what it would be like, so we packed every piece of clothing we had. If mother could have brought her kitchen, I believe she would have packed that too. After we grabbed our suitcases, we went to look for my father. Even though it had only been two months since he left, it seemed longer to me because I had been living away in Kingston.

There he was. His tall stature was easily visible, and I recognized him over the crowd by the airport door. The door opened, and he barged in. For the first time I saw him embrace and kiss my mother. Mother's reaction was so hilarious. She lifted her hand in shock as if she was being resistant to dada's embrace. My sister and I shied away just a little. We waited for him to notice or hug us too; but he was so ecstatic to have his wife in his arms, I thought he did not notice us. He finally turned toward his young daughters and hugged us.

To be honest I never felt my father's embrace like this before. It was that kind of hug as if he hadn't seen us in an awfully long time. He always portrayed a serious facial expression; but when I reflected on that day, the image of his facial expression was the best. One of my older brothers who was already living in the States was there to greet us as well. On our ride from the airport there were streets that were indeed different from Jamaica. Crowded smooth streets, big buildings, and noise everywhere. I was in awe of this place.

"We in foreign," I whispered to my sister.

"I know," she whispered back as we giggled together in the back seat of my brother's little car.

Upon arriving at a small street in the Bronx, we were greeted by the sound of the subway train above. I had never seen a train or a train track before. Now I was under a train rail. I thought, "Wow, what kind of America is this?" It was about 9:30 P.M. when we pulled up to the mid-rise building which was a part of a cluster of mid-rise buildings. The smell of cigarette smoke combined with the smell of food traveled up my nose. It was clear there were a lot of people living there. A mixture of loud music and chatter bounced from different sections of the buildings.

Mother was so happy to be reunited with her husband and to have me back in her presence. We all got out of the car, and my brother went to park. My father told us to wait for my brother to come back. I tossed my book-bag on my back while we waited. I didn't understand this method of "parking the car." There were cars lined all up and down the street. My brother came walking back towards us with such a happy look on his face. Seeing my older brother felt brand new to me because when I was growing up, he was never around. By the time I was born, he was already an adult living on his own.

He came towards me.

"Stacy," he said as he gave a big smile and I laughed with him.

My brother grabbed two of the suitcases and pulled them toward the door of the dingy building while my dad pulled two more. I guess that was where we would spend the night. My brother took one step inside the small entry way and pressed a button. Then there was a loud buzzing sound.

"But my gawd," said mother as they pushed the door open.

We moved further into the building, and my brother pressed another button on this small red door. We all crammed in what they called an elevator.

I now understood why it is called foreign; because believe me, everything there was totally foreign to me—a parked car, buzzing door, elevator, train rails, and buildings as tall as nothing I've ever seen. Good God, what else is there in this place that will amaze me? Well, there was always something. We got out of the elevator, passed two brown doors, and then we all stood in front of one. My brother pressed another button. The thought of pressing all these buttons had become intriguing to me. What else can we press a button to do in this America? The door opened to reveal the welcoming smiles of a bright faced lady, which turned out to be my sister in-law, and another one of my brothers. My sister and brother shouted, "Wahoo," and whatever else patois phrases came from their mouths with excitement. I don't even know if I said anything, but I gave off so much laughter.

The sound of happiness filled that apartment. This was one of my happiest moments in life. Turns out it not only was where I would sleep for the night, but it was where I would spend the next three years. It would be my first home in America. The place I would learn so many valuable lessons and where my parents would stay until the day they died.

CHAPTER 10

The High School Years

𝓘t was the summer of 1990 in New York City. Schools were closed for the summer break, and here I was in America looking for the milk and honey I've always heard about. It was noisy, busy, and dirty. I was used to seeing my neighbors in their yards, barking dogs, chickens, and even stray cats. These neighbors here in America were extremely close, almost on top of each other. My family and I shared a one-bedroom apartment. There were six of us knitted like a blanket inside this tiny apartment with only two beds. At least in Jamaica we had a little more living space.

There was no longer any going outside to play in the yard, picking fresh fruit, or wandering into a secret place under a tree. I was in a tall building looking through a couple of small windows only to see and hear trains passing by day and night. Sirens went off just about every second, and the other building blocked my view of all that was next to us. The sound of loud music and talking drummed every day, and it just seemed as if no one slept in this neighborhood. June finished and the temperature had the tiny room extremely hot. We had one fan. It would sit in the living/bedroom when we all sat down for dinner, but after that the fan would go in my parents' room. July creeped in and the hot temperature seemed hotter.

We all wanted to go outside, but there were no neighboring friends' houses to go visit. So, we were locked up in the house like prisoners. I was curious to know where the trains were going and what else was outside, hoping I would find a fruit tree or something to remind me of Jamaica. A few evenings my sister in-law would come by and we'd babysit my niece and nephew but still didn't go outside. One Saturday when my sister in-law came to visit us with her children, she decided to take us outside to walk around and see the streets of the Bronx. We hurried and got dressed in our little ragged clothes from Jamaica.

There were so many people all different complexions out there on the corners and in the stores. There were a lot of Puerto Ricans.

I wondered, "Could it only be Puerto Ricans that lived among us, and we are the only Jamaicans here besides my other family members?"

My sister in-law took us to the main shopping center close to the house, and since it was hot, she offered to buy us "ice" from the man with his cart.

He stood saying, "Coco, Coco."

What does that even mean? The man's cart reminded me of the "fudgy man" I used to enjoy in St. Andrew. All of us including my niece and nephew stood in line in the hot sun.

"Coco, rainbow, limon or cherry," the man with a deep accent asked.

I did not know what to pick so I opted for the red one. I think we all got the red one except for my mother. She was skeptical about eating food or anything from outside her kitchen, especially on the road.

"Grandma tastes it," my niece stretched up her hand.

Mother barely put her mouth to it and said with her finger she did not want any more. Little did I know this was the traditional summer cool-down treat for the children and adults alike.

Before we knew it August came, and summer was over. We were introduced to Aunt Gwen, who came to get my sister and I so we could register for high school. Her dedication to us was so amazing. She held our hands and introduced us to "Summer in the Bronx," which included the high school we would attend in September. It was the biggest building I had ever seen, Dewitt Clinton High School. Parents and students went in and out from every side. As Aunt Gwen walked us inside the school, she pleasantly greeted the administrator.

"Good morning, my name is Gwendolyn Scott, and these are my two lovely nieces. They just came from Jamaica, and I would like to register them for September."

She spoke so eloquently and dressed so classy. She reminded me so much of Claire Huxtable. I developed such an admiration for her.

Little did I know September was not far off, and there were no uniform measurements the way my mother did in Jamaica. I had to wear regular clothes to school. That was different. Not sure how that was acceptable in America, but I had to follow the rules. The second Monday in September I got ready for my first day of school in America. I was a shy, pretty, little girl with a deep Jamaican accent. I had on a tee shirt and jeans from Conway, sneakers from Payless, a colorful book bag on my back, and my fully gelled up thick jheri curls. I stood next to my sister as we looked up at the big school building in front of us.

My heart was pounding. I felt as if my jheri curls had started dripping on my neck. I glanced at my sister's face and her facial expression was so serious. She had that ready, set, go fight face. I felt protected looking at her as I had an instant flashback to the boys she had bombarded on my behalf a couple years back. I pulled up my bag straps knowing my sister was ready to come to my aid if necessary.

As I made it to the first step, I went into instant culture shock. I just wanted to go back home and sit with my parents. I had never seen so many students in one school, much less a school so big. There were so many different languages being spoken at the same time. It was amazing. How was I going to adjust to this kind of lifestyle? I don't remember seeing anything like this on the TV, and nobody warned or prepared me for this. The Cosby Show only showed their family in their home or their children coming in from school. They never showed what the school setting was really like. I felt deceived by the way television in Jamaica had depicted America to me.

Back during the summer, I had met Aunt Gwen's son Marcus. I found out he was attending the same school with us. I walked into that school with the intention to be the best student from Jamaica, but the busy hallways, different teachers and classrooms intimidated me. I searched all over the crowded school grounds to spot my cousin Marcus, but he was nowhere to be found. Soon my searching came to a halt. The lunch bell rang, and everyone scattered to the lunchroom. I took my time trying to familiarize myself with the classrooms and bathrooms. When I finally found the cafeteria, it seemed as if I was the last one to enter.

I gathered my lunch from the stout lady in her black hair net, then surveyed the room for a seat. Everybody was busy chatting in their cliques. Somehow, I was glad they didn't notice me. I spotted an empty seat and took my little tray with my mashed potatoes, corn puffs with a tiny box of chocolate milk, and sat down. I felt so alone. It was not the first time I felt alone, but this time it seems as if my loneliness was obvious. A boy came over and tried to hold a conversation with me, but that didn't go well, or maybe it did. My cousin Marcus showed up.

He said, "Yo, that's my little cousin, leave her alone."

I was so happy to see him. He became my bodyguard from then on just as my brothers were when I was in Jamaica. Even though my sister went there, sometimes I would only see her at dismissal. We'd bump into each other as we tried to make it home to catch the daytime soap operas, One Life to Live and General Hospital. As I reflect on those days, it was fun after I finally blended in.

One of the most challenging times I had was learning to speak Spanish. This struggle resulted in me becoming very antisocial which lowered my self-esteem and self-confidence. The thought of learning Spanish scared me because of how I sounded speaking it with my Jamaican accent. All this put a strain on me. I started comparing myself to other students in other areas. The way they spoke and dressed began to make me feel uncomfortable around them. The fight to belong took its toll on me. Why didn't these students see this and allow me to be a part of their cliques? I came from a good family, had respect, and didn't want to fight anyone. Many days I would get teased about my accent, the way I mispronounced words, and the fact that my clothes were not like their fancy name brands. Who would've thought America was this cold?

November came and it was freezing. If someone had told me foreign was a freezing place, maybe my excitement to come here would have been less. My sister in-law introduced us to the different stores that sold winter gear.

I was astonished by this "winter gear." First, we went to get thick coats, thick socks, scarves, hats, and gloves. Then we'd go to Payless and Fabco shoe stores to get boots with fur like material inside and high up our ankles.

"Yuh toes will freeze up if yuh don't wear these kinds of socks and besides, it go get colder. Oonu wait until it starts snow," my sister in-law would say.

I came to realize there was no preparation for this at all. I was used to being barefoot, wearing slippers or regular shoes, and my little frilly nylon socks for church and school.

Our first Thanksgiving Day came, and the family got dressed up in our warm clothing and went to Aunt Gwen's for dinner. Oh my God, mother always cooked for us, but when we arrived for dinner at Aunt Gwen's nice big house and saw the amount of food on the table, I was shocked.

"A wah dat," we asked looking at the turkey on the tray.

We had chicken in Jamaica, and this turkey sure wasn't like any chicken we'd seen before. Aunt Gwen later explained the turkey to us, as well as the traditional meaning behind such a feast and holiday. It was such a beautiful family gathering, and I got to meet more cousins as they welcomed us to America. Being with family for this occasion reminded me of Christmas in the country of St. Andrew, where story time with laughter filled the room, such joy and love in the sweetest way.

Talking about Christmas, right before December 25th the phone rang.

The caller said, "Look through the window, it a snow."

Mother, with a smile on her face, called out to my sisters and I with the message. There were a couple of small windows in the apartment, and I ran to the one in my parents' room while one of the sisters looked out from the living room window and my oldest sister looked out the kitchen window. It was amazing to watch this soft cotton like substance fall from the sky. Outside of one of the windows was what they called a fire escape, and all that snow landed on it and created a mountain of pure white fuzz. I wanted to touch it just to fulfill my curiosity.

Someone yelled from across the way, "It's snowing!"

My oldest sister had the brilliant idea that we should go outside instead of looking through the window. The temperature was 31 degrees, and we had to bundle up in layers of clothing with our heavy boots. By the time we got dressed and made it outside, the snow was already piled up by the entrance of the building. We dashed out of the building and onto the sidewalk. We took turns taking pictures of our first snow. If we did not have any stories to tell our family and friends back in Jamaica, we sure had this one with pictures to prove it. Mother had refused to step out in snow, but her face showed every ounce of excitement as she watched her children's reaction.

I said, "Bow, you should come feel it, it is so soft," as I gathered a bit in my hand from the parked cars.

There were so many children outside filled with joy playing in the snow as it fell like a blanket over us. The more the snow was coming down the more excited they became. Some were playing ball with it, while some of the adults had their little children in containers pulling them up and down the sidewalk. The children had on so many clothes you could barely see their eyes. After a while, mother shouted for us to come inside. As we got inside and took off all our winter gear, she prepared tea and crackers for us. That snow lasted for days. School was closed, and we could barely see the cars and the street. It was piled so high it probably came halfway up my leg if I had stepped in it. There was no intention to go back out there until it cleared up.

All those days of snowy weather dampened mother's spirit, and all she wanted from that moment on was to go back to Jamaica to be in the sun and on her farm. Who could blame her? This was not inviting or fun, but there was no talk of us going back to Jamaica. So, I was not entertaining the thought. Days of looking at the bright sunshine and enjoying its warmth on our face were a distant memory. We were now living in the extreme opposite. The fluffy snow had now become ice on every surface it was once laid on, and that was even worse. Once school did re-open, I had to be more careful than usual because there were invisible ice patches or ice patches that blended in with the ground. All my across the street to school days were over, at least for now.

In Jamaica, cold times were only at night, but in America it was all day and night for months. I just could not accept this kind of cold and extra clothes. My little size was being weighed down by the extra layers of clothes, but there was nothing I could do. It was either that or be cold, and I chose the clothes. I couldn't stand the cold in the hills of St. Andrew, and this American cold was different. It would sting you. Sometimes my eyelashes felt as if they were frozen and about to fall off. The thought of writing to my friends in Jamaica and telling them not to come here if they didn't want to experience this kind of cold ran through my mind.

After all those winter months, spring came, and it finally warmed up. Then came my favorite time of year in America, summer. I got my first job in the Summer Youth program as a cashier at Yankee Stadium. I was happy, so incredibly happy knowing I would have my own money to buy some better clothes. Another good thing about this job was it allowed me to socialize more which was something I had struggled with since coming to America. My job had required me to interact with them, so I had no choice. Either I pretend to have high self-esteem or just let their presence boost my confidence. At the end of the week my paycheck was a mere $60, but I was so happy and proud that I had earned money for myself to buy new clothes for the upcoming school year. Each paycheck I bought more clothes and sneakers. They were not like the fancy ones the other kids had, but they were better than what I started out with. Come September, I was going to be a better version of myself.

During my time working at Yankee Stadium, I met so many different people from all sorts of nationalities which boosted my self-esteem. When the new school year came around, I felt a sense of confidence when I walked in that school building in my new clothes, new book bag and sneakers. A few of the students who had mocked me before kept going at it again, but because I made a few adjustments the teasing did not really affect me so bad this time around. My whole intent was to refocus my mind on my school lessons and persevere.

My father's voice echoed in the back of my head, "Learn your lesson."

In Biology, I sat across from this handsome boy. Good Lord, he was so good looking and seemed very smart too. He was so focused on the teacher, but I was focused on him. Every glance at him made me hot even on the coldest days and caused my heart to beat faster than usual. The stares became more frequent as I tried to convince myself that I would introduce myself to him, but then I shied away. Each day in class I became fixated on my thoughts of him hoping he would look at me, but he didn't; or maybe he did when I was not looking. My belief was that he did look at me and probably was just as shy as I was. How could he not notice me? I stood out like a thorn on a rose bush as the new, fair skin, slender girl with the Jamaican accent, and thick jheri curls.

In the first week during Spanish class, I met one of the sweetest girls in the school. I thought she was so pretty with her long black hair and fair skin. Her eyes were so caring, and she never looked at me with prejudice. It was a multi-cultural school so there was a variety of students with different complexions. Capri Navas, (Rest In Peace), was from Guadalupe, and on that bright September day we sat next to each other.

She smiled at me and whispered, "What's your name?"

I replied, "Avis."

I knew I had a new friend as my smile broadened. After Spanish class dismissed, we checked our schedule and realized all our classes were scheduled together. What a great way to build a friendship and not feel alone anymore. It was the best thing to happen to me in that big school.

Days when Capri and I didn't want to eat in the lunchroom we would walk to the local deli across the street. There was no extra money for me to spend on a bag of chips. My lunch money was $2 - $5. On those days I bought chicken wings and fried rice with a soda from the Chinese restaurant that was it for my lunch money. But Capri would get me a bag of potato chips knowing I didn't have any more money. She was so kind to me. Most of the time during lunch I would rush home for lunch, only because I lived five minutes away from school.

Mother would cook up some hot dogs or Vienna sausages plastered with ketchup on a piece of bread or over white rice. Then I would wash it down with some kool-aid or fresh squeezed lemonade and go back to school. Occasionally I would be late for school because I was home playing with the baby boy my mother was babysitting, or I would get caught up in one of the famous daytime soap operas. Capri and I remained friends right through high school. As a matter of fact, she was my only friend until I met another girl my senior year. Our goals were similar and with my deep Jamaican accent and her deep Spanish accent, we were like global sisters.

We had funny days where she wanted to sound like me, and I wanted to sound like her. Those days usually turned out funnier than what we expected. I became less shy during our final year of high school. Neither one of us had a prom date, not because no one asked, but we had a naive way about us and shied away from any potential guys. Unfortunately, the nice-looking boy from biology class never asked me. We went to the prom with the new girl, and the three of us got a limo and had a great time. My dear friend Capri and I planned to attend the same College, Niagara University. We became inseparable during those years and off to Niagara we all went. My decision to attend Niagara was simple and based on one thing. I felt if I attended a predominantly white institution, there would be less distractions and it would be quiet compared to the noisy high school and neighborhood where I lived. I expected to get my first degree in America. I kept my focus, and my expectation became a reality.

CHAPTER 11

The College years

It was August 1994, two months after graduating high school. I took on responsibility for myself, and just like that I was an instant adult. I left my parent's tiny apartment to move 14 hours away at Niagara University in Niagara Falls, New York. I thought I had culture shock in High School. No, this was a hard reality check to the core of my being. I was now surrounded by more white people than I had ever seen, except for on television. Most of the time I was the only black student in my class. This prompted me to become more competitive and less intimidated by my surroundings.

Failing was not an option for me. I did not want to be

teased or mocked by these students. So, working harder was my remedy. Then, I wanted to make my parents, especially my dad, proud of me.

He said, "Don't waste my money," when he dropped me off on campus.

Whenever I found myself struggling, I used help from every resource at my disposal for my schoolwork and emotional support. The struggle to maintain my grades was real. No matter how hard I tried, it seemed as if my grades were not improving.

The thought of falling behind became devastating and discouraging to me. My hope of being the best student was quickly unraveling with the pressure of life. I felt myself slipping into a dark state, but as often as I could, I whispered a small prayer to God asking him to help me achieve my goal and to not let me embarrass myself or my father. I wanted to do right by my father. I wanted to make him proud. He never made it this far in his education, and being his last child, I wanted his heart to smile at my accomplishment.

Amid my last year of college, I rededicated my life to my Lord and Savior Jesus Christ thanks to an African American girl I met around campus. One Sunday, she invited me to a church service, and the spirit of God moved so viciously in that place. People were getting delivered from all infirmities and demonic entanglements. I too got delivered from the dark forces that had surrounded me. I was now drawn to the Spirit of God once more.

Church was a normal thing for me from a tender age. What was the difference you ask? See, growing up I saw the relationship my parents and those in the community had with the Lord, and my earlier relationship with God was based on their experiences. This time it was deeply personal, and that was new to me. I took the invitation as a sign that it was time to go back into a congregational setting which is what I was used to and enjoyed. The services got better and better as I started to attend more frequently. Little did I know this was a path being prepared by God for the great work he had in store for me.

Not too long after, I received an opportunity to do an internship in Washington DC as a women's counselor. The city was beautiful and filled with beautiful black people which made me at home. While there I applied to Howard University for their master's program. I got accepted on a probationary status because of my low GPA from Niagara University. The advisor warned me, in order to stay in the program, I needed a GPA of 3.0 or higher. Well, I took that to mean I only needed five points. Nope, not so. I had to work harder than ever before. I was determined not to be a failure and to prove to my parents I was not wasting time or their money in college. I also did not want to go back to New York.

I refocused and shifted my mindset into another gear. I loved it in Washington, DC. Everyone there was on the move as they tried to carry out their goals and missions. It wasn't as busy as New York City, but it wasn't as slow as

Niagara either. The pace of things ignited my mind and heart in such a way that I developed a drive to succeed even more. My confidence and dedication became my amour as I learned the importance of "bouncing back." Once again, whatever I lacked, I found a resource to help me. By the time graduation came, I had a G.P.A of 3.5, and by the grace of God I graduated on time. The news made it home to my parents that I had completed my schooling and was graduating.

The word graduation meant a lot to them. It was a sign that we were not poor in education. They never wanted any other negative label on their family. I was so grateful I got the opportunity to graduate and have my family in attendance. The look on my family's face when the ceremony was over was priceless. "Stacy, congratulations," rolled off their lips and made my heart merry; however, the moment was bittersweet.

Capri was scheduled to graduate with me, but she suddenly died a month before graduation. I was so heartbroken. This was the first time I had ever experienced such pain. The pain of losing someone so close was devastating. She was my first friend in America and to lose her so unexpectedly took a deep toll on me. I promised myself that whatever I did from that point on would be to honor Capri's memory.

IN AUGUST 1998, I returned to the city of Washington, DC to attend graduate school at one of the most prestigious Historical Black Colleges, Howard University, and to complete a great internship program. For my first semester, I interned at The Salvation Army as a Case Manager. The thought of wanting someone close to me crossed my mind on several occasions. As time went by, the yearning for a husband became more of a strong desire, especially when I walked away from the public and closed the door behind me at night. I never had a boyfriend growing up or during my college years. You could say I had never been kissed. Well, I was almost kissed.

When I was in high school, I really liked this particular boy that asked me out on a date. Mother of course didn't approve of such things so I couldn't share this with her. Although it was uncharacteristic of me, I lied to mother. I told her I was going to the library, but instead I went over this boy's house. I got to his house feeling all nervous because I had never done anything like this before. As we sat on his couch talking, he leaned over to kiss me. His breath met my nose before his lips met mine. It smelled so bad I just couldn't go through with it. I hopped up and ran out of there. I guess it served me right because I had no business being there in the first place.

The urge for companionship at this place in my life led me to earnestly start praying for a husband. I was specific with my prayer request and asked God to give me someone after his own heart. I didn't want to date several men and then have to choose or live-in fornication. My whole life I had always been surrounded by married couples living together. Living any other lifestyles seemed out of order to me.

So, my prayer was extremely simple, "Lord, the first man I date, please let him be my husband."

Well, God heard my prayers and gave me just what I asked for.

It was an extremely hot day on the campus of Howard University. I had just finished my internship for the day and was walking across campus. I saw this well-built man dressed in a black suit with deep black sunshades and a briefcase swinging in his hand walking toward me. I was a bit intimidated by his appearance as he approached. I became nervous and put up my defenses as we were within inches of each other. He stopped and shifted out of the way. I hurried past him.

With a deep weird accent he asked, "How you doing?"

I quickly responded, "I'm doing fine, are you saved," as I kept walking.

I knew if I asked him if he was saved, I would not come off as an easy target. Besides, I was not impressed by his presence in that all black attire and those dark sunshades where I couldn't even see his eyes.

His strong voice responded, "I am above fantastic, and looking at your beautiful face made me feel more fantastic. You are very pretty."

I slowed my pace as he walked up beside me. My spirit quickened which left my heart to pump a bit faster with a rush of extra heat under my long flowing summer skirt. I was startled by the quickening as he continued with the conversation.

I tried to dismiss the extra pumping of my heart and block out his conversation at the same time. It was my survival tactic. I did not have time to get caught up with this man. Nevertheless, I stopped.

Smiling I said, "Thank you."

He stretched his hand out to shake mine. I hesitated out of fear. I didn't know this man or his intent. I didn't want to be snatched up by a stranger in the streets of Washington DC. I held on to my bag with one hand and restrained my other hand by my side.

"My name is Doug. What's your name," with his speech getting faster he continued, "I'm coming from the chapel. I'm a keyboard player. Do you work around here?"

The thought of answering him was easy. I wanted to end the conversation, get away from him, and go home hoping he would not follow me. I was not going to be deceived by his fancy talk.

My Jamaican accent rolled out, "No. Actually I am a student here. How come I never seen you before?"

He smiled.

"You don't believe me? Well, I don't blame you. I'm just a strange keyboard player trying to hold a conversation with an angel. But it's okay," he said as he shrugged his shoulders.

This was my chance to stop the conversation and move on, but before I knew it the conversation went on.

He tickled my emotions with different keyboard stories.

"What was your name again?" He asked.

I laughed and said, "I never told you my name, but it's Avis."

I finally shook his hand.

"Nice to meet you," he said.

The grip from his manly hand electrocuted my heart, and the heat I felt earlier returned rushing all over my belly. He never took off his glasses, and even though I had a little suspicion, I trusted my internal spirit knowing he meant me no harm. He finally let go of my hand, as we stepped off in opposite directions.

Turning away, I blushed with a smile on my face. After a few steps, I glanced over my shoulder and our eyes met as he turned to look back at me at the same time. He quickly walked back.

In his fast-speaking tone he said, "Can I have your number?"

With no hesitation, I gave my phone number to this stranger dressed in full black. No man had my number, but I wanted to see where this smooth-talking man' intentions were. He took my number and walked away promising to call.

That very night he called me, and we talked far into the night about the goodness of God. The conversations between us prolonged from days to weeks, then weeks to months as he had now become a mentor of the scriptures to me. My heart was filled with gratitude for having this man take the time to teach me the scriptures every night. His knowledge of the bible had caught my attention and stirred up the level of my spirituality. He had prophetic gifts and an anointing that ignited my gifts of healing, encouragement, and preaching of the gospel. I had longed to find someone that would mentor me on this.

Months into our phone calls, we became more comfortable with each other. We usually ended our calls with him praying, but this one night before he started praying, he asked me out on a date. As I shared before, I'd never gone out on a date before. So being the shy young lady I was, I wrestled with the answer in my mind. I didn't even know what to expect or what to wear. Before answering him, I put the phone down, hurried to my tiny closet, and surveyed all my "church clothes." Since he was a "church man" I figured whatever my choice of clothing would be appropriate. I realized he might have hung up the phone during my delay in answer while searching my closet, but he didn't.

"Hello," I said as I placed my dress in my lap.

"Yes, I'm still here. So, what you say I pick you up on Friday evening about 7 P.M.," he responded.

The thought of going on my first date made me smile.

I responded, "Ok."

Friday evening, when he came to pick me up, he gave me a tight hug with my chest pressed up against his broad chest. Black must have been his favorite color because he was dressed in yet another black suit. I felt a flutter as I looked him over. He took me to this little restaurant in downtown DC. While in the car he glanced over at me.

He said, "You are really pretty."

Blushing I said, "Thank you."

By this time, a nervousness began to flood my mind and I was trying to relax. We pulled up to our destination, and as I was about to unbuckle my seat belt, he came around to my side and opened the door for me.

He said, "Don't you touch that door," as he stretched his hand to escort me out of the car.

We marched towards the restaurant's door, and he held it open for me to enter. He was such a gentleman. Once in the restaurant, we were escorted to our table. He waited patiently as me and my big pocketbook slid into the quaint booth. He was such a gentleman the entire night. I don't remember much about the food we ate because I was so captivated by his presence. Just looking at him across the table sent warm feelings throughout me. I had so many questions running through my mind. Was God answering my prayers? Could this be the husband and companion I'd been awaiting?

After our dinner, we returned to the car headed home. Honestly, I didn't want the night to end. We pulled up outside my building. He again jumped out to come and open my car door. We walked to the door.

He turned to me and said, "So, now that we've made it through our first date, would you like to go to church with me on Sunday?"

He attended Emmanuel Church of God in Christ

where he was a minister and keyboard player. I didn't really know if that would be our second date or just us going to church together, but I gladly accepted his invitation. This would help me to see him in action and learn more about his role in the church, as well as his skills on the keyboard. I was not a professional singer, but I knew how to carry a tune and build some rhythm in a song. So, I thought with him being a keyboard player and I a somewhat singer was the perfect combination.

From that one Sunday I became a regular member of the congregation accompanied by Minister Douglas Wych II every Sunday. At Emmanuel Church of God in Christ I discovered what having a close relationship with God looked like and developed a close personal walk with God. I had the opportunity to know and experience the love of God even more. Although I spent my early years in the church, there was knowledge of God but a lack of understanding of what a real relationship with God meant. Here I learned what it meant to fall in love with Jesus.

This was an exciting time in my life, because being away from my family without a church home was lonely at times. I wanted spiritual stability while I obtained my degree, and this gave me a way to do so. Doug and I became closer and spent more time together. There was no doubt in my mind that he was in fact my husband and the man I prayed for. Month after month, Doug faithfully picked me up and made sure I attended Friday night Bible studies and Sunday morning services. I remember one

Sunday, the Pastor, Pastor Donnell Smith, pulled me to the side.

He said, "I can see the hand of God strongly in your life."

It wasn't hard for me to believe him because I felt it too. It felt like such a strong anointing over me which caused me to feel powerful in all I set out to do. My confidence in Christ increased and I started to invite students from Howard University to attend services on Sundays. In no time, I formed a College Christian Ministry on campus which spread to the streets of Washington DC as I began to minister to the homeless. The power of the Holy Ghost was strongly empowering me everywhere I went and was noticeable every time I laid my hands on someone to pray for them. As a result, they would receive the Holy Spirit with the evidence of speaking in different tongues, and then I knew God had equipped me for his glory and purpose.

CHAPTER 12

The Longest Summer

Summer break in May 1999, I wanted to return to my family in New York. It had been a while since I was home, and I was excited. I met up with Doug one evening and shared my plans to spend the summer with my family in New York. To my surprise, he broke down and cried as he held on to me.

He said, "No! Oh my God really? I am going to miss you. Things have to change. I will make sure you have your own place. I just don't want you to leave me."

I started crying too because we had such a connection, and I didn't want to leave him either. However, there was nowhere for me to go for the summer since school was closed. Besides, I missed my family a great deal, especially my mother's cooking. So, after all that crying, hugging, and smooching between us my decision was clear. I had to go to my family.

While I was home with my family, I had a clear vision where God showed me that upon my return to Washington, DC, Doug was going to propose. I tried to prepare my heart for what was forthcoming, hoping I was ready. The uncertainty of a proposal lingered in my head. I wasn't sure if I was even ready for marriage even though I had prayed for a husband. Wanting to be married and being ready to be married were two different things. I debated within myself. Then I remembered the the request I made to God.

"Let the first man I go on a date with be my husband."

Sharing this kind of stuff was not normal in the family or among the church members and leaders. So, I kept my feelings bottled up inside with the hope of returning to Washington, DC to talk to Doug about the matter.

Cell phones were not prevalent back then and to make a long-distance call cost money, which I did not have. Missing Doug weighed heavily on me as I constantly counted the days until we'd be together again. Waiting the entire summer was draining and seemed as if we were separated for a year. The thought of getting back to DC and in Doug's company gave me a different kind of feeling, the feeling of wanting his presence. He was a gentle soul with me. I'd never experienced feelings like that before, and I wanted to continue feeling them with this man. I felt there was a divine connection between us and wanted to share how I felt with him.

Summer ended and it was finally time to return to D.C. Doug picked me up from the Greyhound bus station and neither of us could contain our excitement to see each other. When we hugged, he held on to me like he never wanted to let go. We had so much to tell each other, that car certainly had no peace during that ride. The following weekend he came to get me just for an evening walk. We held hands and strolled past the small body of water as the ducks swam in their little group. It was beautiful to watch them. Suddenly Doug let my hand go and went down on one knee. He gently took hold of my left hand.

Looking up into my eyes, he said, "Will you marry me?"

Unconsciously I snatched my hand from him as they anxiously shook covering my mouth. My heart raced as my breath met its pace to form a musical rhythm.

"Is that a yes?"

Instantly I responded, "Yes, yes, yes!!!"

I tried to relax as the tears rolled down my cheeks. I took a couple of deep breaths.

Then I shouted, "Yes, I will marry you!"

Now, why was I shocked? God had already showed me he was going to propose. The diamond ring went on my finger, and it felt like the marriage ceremony had already happened. He stood up and gave me a juicy kiss and lifted me up off the ground. We both were elated in the moment. We laughed later because it was a struggle for him to get up from the kneeling position.

I did not tell anyone about my engagement, but to my surprise a few days later I received a phone call from a close friend from New York.

She said, "You are going to get married."

I burst out laughing. Little did she know I was already engaged, but I wasn't telling her that. I needed to break the news to my family before I told anyone else. It was a hard secret to keep though. Visions and dreams of our wedding flooded my mind every night. In one of the dreams, I saw a big beautiful building where my reception would take place.

Someone said, "I will pay for the reception."

As I woke up from the dream, I could not for the life of me figure out who that person was. Nevertheless, in my spirit I was on the lookout for them.

In my family, it was customary to take your fiancé to meet your parents. We'd kept our secret for months. So, Doug and I decided it was finally time for him to go to New York to meet my parents and the rest of the family. It was Thanksgiving so the timing was perfect. Doug had never been to New York, but the anxiety of meeting my parents outweighed the excitement of his first visit to the city. He was aware of my firm Jamaican upbringing and was intimidated by the reputation of my dad.

I called my dad and told him the plan and purpose for my trip. Our four-hour ride to the city was exciting, well at least for me. Doug was worried and praying hard my father would approve of our relationship and engagement. The more I tried to reassure him everything would turn out fine, the more the sweat beads popped up on his forehead. We arrived at my parent's home, and my dad greeted us at the door. As Doug entered the apartment, my dad reached out and shook his hand.

In his deep Jamaican accent he said, "This is my baby girl, my last child."

He tightened his grip on Doug's hand as he spoke.

Nervously Doug looked him in the eye and replied, "Yes, sir. I understand, I will take very good care of her. I promise."

My mother smiled and of course offered Doug something to eat. Meanwhile, my dad continued with his inquiries.

Doug was like an open book. He explained to my father that he was divorced with two children. My father cleared his throat and leaned back in his chair.

"So where is your wife, sir," he asked.

Doug's nerves now transferred to me as he explained to my father where his ex-wife and children were. I wondered what my father would say after hearing that news, but to my surprise he looked at me.

"Stacy, are you sure this is from God?" he said with a bold voice.

I confidently answered, "Yes."

"If this is what you want then God be with you."

Mother overheard the conversation on her way back from the kitchen. As she served them a plate of rice and peas with oxtail, she stared at Doug. As she took her seat next to him, my father began to paraphrase the story of Doug's divorce and children for her.

She hummed then said, "Well you were a member of the church here, so you betta go speak to the Pastor."

Doug returned to D.C. without me. I stayed behind and scheduled a meeting with the Pastor of the local church. After 30 minutes of discussion with the Pastor, he informed me I couldn't marry Doug because it was not doctrinal. What was not doctrinal, you ask? He assured me it was not doctrinal for a divorced man to be remarried unless his wife was deceased. I respected his opinion and was so disappointed. Here I was baring my soul to him about a man I knew God sent to be my husband, and he was talking to me about doctrine. I knew God had granted me what I had asked for when I met this man, and there was no question that it was divine order that we get married.

Hurt, I returned to the church the following Sunday. There was a whisper in my spirit to speak with one of the older ladies in the church, what you would call a "Mother of Zion." I quietly spoke with her and shared the whole scenario including the discussion I had with the Pastor. She was so concerned and had such a passion for the young people. She wanted to see them serve God and be married. As I shared with her how I felt, she pulled me to the side.

She quietly said, "They might not believe in certain

things, but if you and this man heard from God, then that is who you must always listen to."

I will remain grateful to this Mother of Zion as her words penetrated the core of my spirit and assured me to go forth with my decision to marry Doug. I learned from that day on to continue listening and hearing God for myself.

CHAPTER 13

Love and Marriage

From the time I met Doug, he was one of my biggest supporters. He leased my first apartment for me, so I didn't have to worry about campus living. He helped me write some of my school papers, and when I felt discouraged or stressed with the work, he would encourage me.

He often reminded me, "You're smart. Listen and trust me when I say I believe in you. I know you can do this; and guess what, I'm not going anywhere."

I believed and trusted him too. Even to the extent that I allowed him to cook some scrumptious American soul food dishes for me. Even though I wasn't in Jamaica anymore, I didn't eat just anyone's cooking.

Even though wedding plans were in full effect, I never shared with him the dreams I had concerning our wedding. We decided to shop around for venues, and surprisingly the first building we went to turned out to be the same building I saw in the dream. He held my hand as we entered the building and whispered to me God had already given him the date. We nervously watched as the wedding coordinator searched her calendar for the date Doug gave her.

She looked up and said, "That date is booked, but I will put your name down in case we have a cancellation."

We believed God, and knew if he said it, so will it be. We continued with wedding plans for July 8th. It was two weeks until our proposed wedding date and still no call from the coordinator. I took matters in my own hands and called her instead. I gave her a simple reminder of who I was and what date we had discussed.

She blurted out, "Oh wow! You're so lucky. That person just called and canceled."

There it was our solid proof that our faith had won once again.

As if that wasn't enough, we had a budget for our wedding of $18,000. That same week someone called me and said he would pay for the wedding full expense without even knowing the total cost. I was grateful to God that we were having our dream wedding without any money from our pockets. God granted us divine favor. I graduated from Howard University with a master's degree in Social Work in May 2000, and on July 8, 2000 I married a man after God's own heart becoming Mrs. Avis Willis-Wych.

* * *

OUR FIRST YEAR of marriage was beautiful. My husband never changed from the original way he treated me. He cooked for me even more and taught me a few of the recipes. He did just about everything to elevate me spiritually and physically. He even taught me how to drive. Our ministry within the church expanded and before long we conceived our first child.

I was in Massachusetts on a speaking engagement and the Lord revealed to me I would conceive a baby girl and three more children thereafter. He told me the pregnancies would be confirmed way in advance before I got to a doctor, and it was so. During one of my sonograms the doctor revealed I was pregnant with a girl. On September 7, 2001, I gave birth to a bouncing baby girl. We named her Naomi which was the name given to me in that same vision that revealed I was pregnant with a girl.

Naomi changed the dynamic of our relationship for the better. Our love for her was so pure. Loving my husband was one thing, but the love I felt when I looked in this baby girl's eyes melted my heart. If you would've told me this kind of love existed, I would've lived my life in great expectation. My baby girl taught me the extent of patience, kindness, love, and purity. Our responsibilities as her parents were heavy, and we were willing to show her what we were made of. It was such an honorable role.

The plan to be better parents than our parents was our primary focus, not that we had bad parents. We both were raised with a solid foundation, especially spiritually. The constant prayers asking God not to let me fail at parenting flowed from my mouth daily. Even though she was in good hands with my husband, my heart was broken on the days when I had to go off to work and leave her. We had rearranged our schedules where I worked daytime and he worked at night. My husband worked harder than ever to provide for us. We lacked nothing, and Naomi was everything to him. She was his first girl, his princess, his heartbeat. The intent to have her groomed in the fear of the Lord was of no question.

Our marital and parental bliss was soon met with a horrifying challenge. I believe one of the most dreadful words anyone hears is, "You have cancer." The very thought of it is scary for the one who has it, but it is also painful for their loved ones. It often seems like a death sentence, but may I tell you this much, that is not always the case.

Seems like it was just yesterday, I was home finishing my daily chores and sat down just to meditate on God. Suddenly, I had this nauseated feeling. It was so bad I ran to the bathroom several times to throw up. The next day the same feeling of nausea rushed my system, and this time my right breast felt extremely heavy. The symptoms I had usually were a sign of pregnancy or PMS. For sure I wasn't pregnant, and I was not on my period. The nausea got worse and so did the vomiting. I thought maybe it was food poisoning, but then I was cooking at home, so how could that be.

It became a major concern after my right breast seemed to get heavier by the day. One evening as I stared at my naked body in the mirror, I lifted my right breast just out of curiosity and noticed a lump. A big lump came in my throat as I looked closely at the lump in my breast. What was that?

Immediately, I thought, "Oh, no!"

I quickly blocked all thoughts of any negative diagnosis out of my head and went on to take my shower. However, I could not bear the pain one more day.

I made an appointment with my doctor and went in for an examination. A day or so later, I sat at home still in pain and prayer. The original lump had now become an abscess. The phone rang and I recognized it was my doctor's office. Sweat started popping up on my forehead.

I answered, "Hello."

"Can I please speak to Mrs. Wych?"

I took a deep breath, "Speaking."

"Your results came back, and I would like for you to come in the office so we can talk about it. Can you come in tomorrow?"

The appointment was confirmed. I got off the phone and told my husband the results had come back, and the doctor wanted me to come in tomorrow. The concerned look on his face only added to mine as we both went into prayer.

While my husband and I sat patiently awaiting the doctor in his office.

My husband said, "Stee, you are going to be fine, I love you."

The doctor's joyous facial expression changed as soon as he sat down at his desk to give me the results.

"Mrs. Wych, the results came back, and the lump is malignant, you have cancer."

My brain immediately went into shock. The only thing I heard was that dreadful word floating in my ears, CANCER. There was no doubt I was in shock, and it probably showed on my face.

The doctor continued, "Mrs. Wych, we have to do surgery immediately."

CANCER. SURGERY. Okay, just wait a minute. How did I get here? A young energetic wife and mother who was caring for her family, to having cancer and needing immediate surgery? I didn't want to accept it. I wasn't going to accept it. I just wanted to wash that whole doctor's visit away and just wake up from this nightmare. But it was clear, this was no dream this time around, it was reality.

After absorbing the news, I went in for the first surgery with the hope that they would not cut off my breast. Even though I was given anesthesia, I could feel every sharp-edged instrument they used. Yes, I felt every move they made under my skin, and the pain soared through my breast tissue. I never understood why they didn't put me to sleep for this procedure. I shouted out to the doctors that I could feel the pain.

Their response was, "We gave you enough anesthesia. The area is numb. You should not be feeling anything."

In my mind I tried to numb the pain as the warm tears trickled down from the corner of my eyes.

I screamed, "Oh my God it hurts!"

For sure God heard me, because somehow, I managed to let the pain put me to sleep. When I opened my eyes, it was all over, and I was in recovery with my breast totally bandaged. Thankfully, when I woke up my breast was still there. Turns out, they drained out the section and sent me on my merry way. Unfortunately, it was not long after before there was a recurrence which required me to return for another surgery. Although I had the two surgeries, the original nausea returned, and so did the same abscess in the same location on my right breast.

It was very puzzling and annoying. I needed to hear from an old familiar voice, so I called one of my sisters. I explained what I was feeling without telling her about any of the previous surgeries.

Concerned she said, "What happened, and how long has this been going on? Are you sure you're not pregnant?"

Again, I knew I wasn't pregnant, so I laughed off her remarks.

She continued, "Umm maybe it's food poisoning or

salmonella. You should go to the infectious disease specialist if that abscess continues."

She was not a nurse, but she had enough medical insight to know a recurring abscess was a sign of something more serious than a pimple on your forehead.

Well, I took her advice. Going to an Infectious Disease Specialist was the best decision I could have made. After several tests, they discovered there was an inflammatory bacteria in my system that had settled in my breast tissue. They gave me several doses of antibiotics, but before the administration of the antibiotics, I underwent a now 6th surgery just to drain out my breast. Thank God after the antibiotic treatment, I had my 7th and final surgery. My body became healed and delivered from breast cancer. No radiation and no chemotherapy, just divine healing from my Heavenly father through the instruments of those knowledgeable doctors.

It was evident that God performed miracles, and he was in control of my life. I underwent seven surgeries in one year, and my God was it a painful experience. During the time of total discharge and home recovery, I had to stretch my praise to God for taking me through. I survived cancer. Yes, I am a cancer SURVIVOR. When I felt better, I wanted to go to church. The bandages were still on my breast, but I went to service anyway and gave a praise dance unto the Lord. I even forgot at one point that my breast was still sore and in bandages. I just knew I owed God that praise. It was that praise that resulted in my total divine healing today. It was my praise that got me out of my pain and suffering.

We remained faithful members of the Emmanuel Church of God in Christ, and in 2004, the Lord called Doug to pastoring. He became the Senior Pastor at Wonder Working Power Church of God in Christ. I served faithfully as his First Lady. A year later, I was ordained as an Evangelist and appointed District Missionary. A year after that I gave birth to my first son Majesty, a name given to him by his father standing for the majestic power of the Almighty God.

Four years into his Pastoral leadership, the family was hit with the sudden and painful passing of Doug's mother. He was devastated by this news. While he tried to accept this loss, it took a major toll on him and he stepped down from pastoring. However, I continued serving the District despite concerns about our spiritual well-being. Doug decided it was best to have us among some strong believers while he got himself together. So, he searched out a congregation that would be a good fit for our family and would pray him through this devastating time of loss. Within a few months, he received a vision of the church we should attend, and he introduced us to the New Community Church of God in Christ.

The congregation was welcoming, but I spent most of the time going there with just Naomi and Majesty. Doug decided staying home grieving was best for him. I still had my mother, so I could not relate to his pain. Nevertheless, I remained his anchor and support partner allowing him to grieve in his own way. I never thought the grieving process would take that long. His grieving went from days to months and then years.

Three years later here comes another precious angel, my baby girl Chosen. Oh Chosen, she was a spitting image of my younger self. Her birth reminded me that I had to be stronger, healthier, and more dependent on God. Chosen was the highlight to the family. Naomi now had a little sister to play with and was so protective of her. She treated Chosen as if she was a doll. Having my three children and my grieving husband as my full responsibility became overbearing.

As much as I adored them all, the burden and struggle were real. Growing up in a huge family had planted the imagery of too many mouths talking and needing to be fed. In all honesty, I never wanted more than one child, and now here I was at number three. Nevertheless, God's plan for my life was going into a different gear, and I dealt with the struggles gracefully being the devoted wife, mother, and head of household. The love I had for my children taught me to love others more with a deep sense of compassion.

Each child had their own personality which added a great flavor to the household. I was grateful to God for blessing me in this role and found the desire for more children. To be fruitful and multiply was now my new vow. The topic of having more children was often discussed, and the fact that I had the dream years back with four children, I was ready. Well, if God granted them to me.

Chosen was only a couple months old when we moved to Connecticut. Doug nor I had close family there, but God had spoken to him and said we were to move there. There was a family friend there that accommodated us for the next five months. During this time God gave me a clear vision of a widow I should attend to. I found the widow God showed me. So, my family moved out and went to live with this widow. When she saw us, she was amazed at the fact that she could have described us in detail as she already saw us in a vision coming to her.

She was a Pastor and invited us to attend a service one Sunday morning. My husband attended, and even played the keyboard for the service. They enjoyed his ministry through music and service was explosive in the spirit. It was at this time little Naomi was filled with the Holy Spirit and the evidence of speaking in tongues right in the basement of this widow's home. This dear widowed Pastor eventually helped us find a two-bedroom place of our own, not too far from her.

We were blessed, and life seemed to be headed in the right direction for us.

CHAPTER 14

In Sickness and In Health

Years had passed and Doug remained depressed over the loss of his mother. Even though we were in a new state away from everything that reminded him of their time together, he was still sad. I learned to trust God when he spoke to my spirit, whether it be a dream, vision, or someone personally speaking to me. We spent several years in Connecticut, and what was a prophetic assignment came to a halt. Now it was time to rearrange our living status and seek God for direction and guidance.

Just when I thought moving was a good decision, my husband started to experience health problems. As a result, in a short time he was hospitalized several times. I wanted to question God as to why the strain on my life, but then I remembered I asked God for a husband. He never promised there would not be any trials, sickness, or troubles. My wedding vows said in health and strength till death do us part, and I was faithful to God as well as my husband.

Doug was diagnosed with Chronic Atrial Flutter. The sound of the word "chronic" hit me hard and devastated me. Here I was in another state hoping to have a better life with my family, and now sickness had invaded our lives. I spent days and nights at the foot of his hospital bed, as I prayed over my husband and pleaded with God not to take him away from me. I could not see myself as a single mother and was not ready to obtain the title of widow at such a tender age.

There were so many times I didn't know how I was going to make it through. There came a day when my son Majesty had a severe asthma attack. It was so bad I thought I was going to lose him. Each breath was frightening as he struggled to breathe and inhale. The thought of those panicked breaths being his last crossed my mind as his eyes piercingly begged me for help. To make matters worse, my husband got admitted to the hospital at the same time. It was double the trouble, but at least they were in the same hospital. It was nothing but the strength of God that held me together because how I managed both in the hospital at the same time was beyond me. As always, I could do nothing but praise God for his healing power. It was tough, but we made it through, and my family came home together.

Unfortunately, not too long after, the stress of life came crashing down. As a result, I experienced several miscarriages. The pain of losing a child more than once scarred my heart. I questioned whether this was a sign that my body had become tired and no longer able to handle the stress. As if that wasn't sign enough, I started to have mini strokes.

I remember one day my left side felt numb and there was a tingling in my hand. Not sure of what was happening and uncomfortable with how I was feeling, I mentioned it to my husband and asked him to take me to the hospital. Upon arrival the nurse took my vitals and saw that my blood pressure was extremely high. They admitted me right away. The doctor came in the room and I explained what I was experiencing.

With no hesitation he said, "Mrs. Wych, you were about to have a major stroke. You did the right thing by coming in."

The doctor's instant advice was to put me on medication so it could be reversed. Months into the medication and several follow-up visits later, I was told the stroke had been reversed. He recommended that I rest and take it easy, otherwise I would have another occurrence. There was no way I could be taken down by a stroke especially dealing with my husband's heart problem and my son's asthma episodes. Who would take care of my family? I praised God daily for being my healer and keeper.

For the next three years life was all figuring out how to care for my husband on every level. Within the fourth year Doug realized the strain on me and that it had become overbearing. So, we made the decision to move back to the Washington, D.C. Metropolitan area. We would stay in Maryland near where the rest of his family was living. This would also allow us to find better medical care and have our children in a stable school system.

Before going back, my husband made arrangements to stay with his best friend for a short time. We both worked on obtaining employment, but matters got worse as we could not find a job. The fear of not having provisions for our family weighed heavy. We always had jobs and resources for our family so the thought of not having them was unnerving. To add to the stress, Doug's best friend pointed out there was too much financial burden on his household, and we had to leave his place. We were now a homeless family of five.

Months before moving I saw my family being homeless in a vision, but there was no way I could accept such a tragedy. I spent days and nights rebuking the vision. I never wanted to see my family homeless. I spent my earlier years ministering to the homeless on the streets, and I knew it was not a pleasant state of mind. With the help of the government, I was able to obtain Temporary Assistance for Needy Families (TANF) and moved into the cheapest Motel 6 paying $59 daily. My husband and I were devastated. We had many sleepless nights with our 3 children and two beds. My world and family were in an uproar.

During that time Tamela Mann's, Take Me to the King, was the song that encouraged me through that rough process. I wept many nights, but I knew God would provide. Our money was exhausted, but God sustained us. My husband received a phone call from his friend who was a Pastor. He told my husband that he had been heavy on his heart and asked if he was ok. With brokenness, my husband was transparent with the Pastor and shared that our family was homeless, and we were out of money to pay for another day.

Graciously, the Pastor said, "Come and stay with us. I have a basement and a bed. It's not in the best condition, but your family is welcome to stay here."

My God, what a relief.

We packed up the few things we had and went to the Pastor's house full of gratitude knowing that God had made a way. In the back of our minds my husband and I knew this was temporary. We were a big family that needed to have our own place. Upon arrival at the promised basement, I was so disappointed.

I thought to myself, "This place doesn't look like we can live in here."

But I caught myself and acknowledged the fact that God made a way for us to at least have some where to lay our heads. I looked around and began turning that basement into a place we could call home.

After a while, the Pastor was shocked at the appearance of his basement and the rearrangements I made.

Purpose was being fulfilled as God used me and my husband to impart knowledge, wisdom, and counseling to that household. Within a few months we were told by the Pastor that one of his family members was suddenly homeless, and it was an emergency for us to move out because he needed the space. At that moment, the Lord gave my husband instructions to reach out to his Aunt who was living in D.C. for help. This was hard, because as a man, his family was in trouble and everything was out of his hands.

While staying at Aunt B's house, the hand of God moved mightily. She was a praying and God-fearing woman. Nevertheless, every day I thanked God for my new job that would allow us to move out of Aunt B's house on our own. My praise through my pain preceded me, and in two months I unexpectedly received a call from an agency offering me a job.

I asked, "How did you find my name and number?"

The representative responded, "We went through our data base and out of thousands your name was highlighted. We would like for you to come for an interview."

I knew that was nothing but God.

My interview was favored and appointed by God because I was offered a job to which I never applied. I now worked at the District Court of Maryland as a Social Worker with a salary that was higher than everyone in my office. This was the job that allowed me to save money while helping Aunt B. Soon we were able to move into our home. Doug and I discussed moving into the suburbs to get out of our bad neighborhood in D.C. We wanted to give our children a better environment with a lesser chance of being gunned down. Well, God took my one income and allowed us to move out of Washington, D.C. to Maryland.

Our home in Maryland was the best and biggest we ever had. Every child had their own room, and it was great. I thought the storm was over, but clearly, I was wrong. Sometime had went by as we settled into our new apartment, Doug was sitting on the sofa and began to moan. I asked what was wrong, and he said his right leg ached so bad. I walked over to him and touched his leg to pray over him. His leg was extremely hot and swollen. I immediately rushed him to the Emergency Room. He could barely walk, but I managed to get him inside and explain to the nurse why we were there. He was admitted, and they discovered a blood clot traveling to his lung. God's timing was perfect. The doctor said had we not made it when we did, my husband would have died. That wasn't the end of the news that day. Doug was also diagnosed with Congenital Heart Failure. My husband's health was declining right in front of my eyes. Even still, he had such a zeal to take care of his family.

I was working full time as a social worker with three young children. So, the new diagnosis affected me quite a bit. Doug had worked for many years as a Special Force police officer; and now because of this medical condition he had to stop working which put an extra strain on me as a sole provider for the family. There were some days he had difficulty breathing even if it was a short distance from the bedroom to the bathroom. The decision to leave his job put a damper on him mentally and physically. He often shared with me during our pillow talk how much he wanted to go back to work. He wanted to live for us.

I would do my best to convince him of how much I needed him. I had vowed to take care of him until death, and I was not seeing "death" just yet for him. I was not seeing death for myself either, so nobody was going anywhere. Taking on the full financial responsibilities for the family was not something I bargained for when we got married, but someone had to do it. The more Doug's health declined, the more it took a toll on his mental state. He felt like less of a man unable to take care of his family. He started to see himself as a failure not only as a man but as a husband and father. The promise he made to my father to take care of his baby girl haunted him day and night.

Devilish thoughts surfaced in his mind and tormented him making him feel unworthy to live. They became more real to him, as he started to believe these thoughts. I would come home from work exhausted and deal with his frustration of failure. Those days when his strength was better, he would cook meals to last for at least two days to help. I spent years watching him struggle with his physical and mental health declining the same.

At night I pleaded with God not to take my husband away from me. My tears had stained many pillowcases as I bawled out to God with the hope of my children not hearing me. Doug tried to comfort me and assure me that he wasn't going to leave me, at least not yet. Every scary thought of him having a heart attack crossed my mind each time we were intimate, but I wanted to trust God to keep him and grant peace for both of us. In my dreams I could sense that my husband would live longer than what the doctors told him.

Finances had now become a burden and my income could no longer sustain the household. The one car we had often broke down. My husband walked miles with me to the bus stop to make sure I was able to get to work. The difficulties of traveling to work on public transportation took a toll on me, and many days I just wanted to quit. Seeing my children's faces every day, as they waited at the door for me to come home gave me something to keep going. The promise of giving them a better life than I had growing up was a promise I had hoped to keep. The struggle was overbearing, but God had sustained us through it all. The decision to switch jobs for better pay was the only choice.

CHAPTER 15

Then There Were Six

I went into another professional field, away from what I knew, to increase my resources to sustain my family's needs. The money was a bit better, but it was not long before they let me go from the position. There went the only income for a household of five. Now what? The first month was okay. I was now spending time with my family, resting, and feeling appreciated. The thought of not having a job never put a strain on the family until the resources were totally exhausted.

My husband's health continued to deteriorate, and life was not the same. As time went on, we struggled to maintain the household expenses. Many times, I had to beg for extensions to pay our rent and for the help from others to feed my children. My mind wrestled with all sorts of how and why God? One year, two years, and half of the third year went by and nothing was changing for my family. Hospital visits for my husband had increased with all the extra strain from the lack of financial resources, and he was not able to help.

I prayed day and night for God to sustain us, and to continue keeping my husband so I would not bear this burden with these young children by myself. I knew God kept me and was sustaining us because every day I looked around my family was still there. The expense of paying rent was high, and once more I had to pack up the family and look for a new living space. We found a smaller space; however, we had to make it work even if we all had to share the same room. I did not want my family separated. So, whatever it took that's what I was going to do.

Within the many years to come, we would move several times. The final straw hit when we lost our townhouse and had to live with someone else. Can you imagine taking your older whole family to live in someone else's house having to adapt once again to their rules and regulations and not wanting to overstay your welcome. They never gave us a timeframe of when to leave. However, one must know staying with someone else with a family of five is not an easy task. Oh, how I missed our house. It was the right size, and it was ours. Losing it was devastating but living with someone else was even more devastating.

Sometimes we must look past what we are facing and

see from a different angle. What we did not know when we first went to live with this lady was that she was getting ready to relocate with a new job position and wanted someone to take care of her house. So, we became her house sitters while she worked in another state. Oh, what a blessing that was. Not worrying about bills for once was heavenly, and my family had a comfortable place to sleep, especially my children. It was an adjustment for them with school, but my heart was so grateful and humble.

Most of my clarity and answers came through dreams and visions. We had been living in this lady's house for a couple of months, and things were looking pretty good. Then one night in a dream, the spirit of God revealed to me that the house was up for foreclosure. Once again, we had to shift gears as the lady came back in town and informed us of the foreclosure. Although we were staying there, our desire was to find a place of our own. Needless to say, we were out in the cold again.

Even though we seemed unstable, my children never once complained. I watched them during the daytime trying to adapt to the constantly changing lifestyle. Thank God they never noticed their parents' tears at night trying to figure out the routine for the next day. It was a vicious cycle getting a place and somewhat stabilizing, only to then have the bills suffocate us and put us back out on the streets. After several attempts to try and catch up with expenses, my husband said we should make payment plans with the bill collectors who were now calling every day. When we couldn't keep up the arrangements, we were back at square one.

Through it all our lights never got cut off. The fridge may have been empty, but we at least had light to read and teach the word of God to the family. Reinforcing what it meant to trust God was our daily task, especially when it was time to feed everyone. I was used to fasting, so going without food was not really a bother to me, but I never wanted to see my children hungry. There was not a doubt that God heard our prayers. While homeless, God blessed us when we needed it the most. Strangers, which I called "angels," came to our place and brought food supplies and clothes for the children. Some days the food was in excess. We had leftovers for two days.

The family didn't mind eating the same food every day. Why would they anyway? It was a blessing from God. Unfortunately, pride kicked in and my husband's thoughts had now become a demon among the family. It was a silent killer that was chewing at the fabric of his mind. Dealing with a heart condition, a war on the mind, and being homeless was not easy. No one would've chosen all of that, I certainly wouldn't have. One night I went to bed crying to God for deliverance, but nothing and I mean nothing came through. Asking for help was like stabbing a sword in my husband's heart. He had so much pride, and well, I guess I had pride too.

We were now in what you'd call "Years of trials." All my children were school age and being dragged around like rag dolls. It was so frustrating. It had now been nine years since I had Chosen, and I became pregnant with my baby boy, Dominion. In February 2017, while in my eighth month of pregnancy we moved into another apartment that seemed fitting for our single income. March 9th, less than a month later, I went into labor. The pain rocked my body. It felt different from the rest of my children. This time it was severe and required more doctors than usual.

The final push to get the baby out came with a serious cry of despair. I'm not sure if it was a cry for God to help me with the labor pain, or for my entire situation. The whole time, my daughter Naomi stood in the room with me in place of my husband. She tried to keep me calm as she video recorded the birth and called to give updates to our family members. Let me tell you just a little about this baby boy Dominion.

The fact that I got pregnant in all that chaos seemed like a miracle all by itself. I wonder sometimes if I should've named him Miracle, but I gave that responsibility to my husband, and he gave him the name Dominion. I guess he wanted someone to represent how God can dominate a situation. The doctors gave him little hope of survival. He was born with a few missing ribs, had to be fed through a tube, and spent the first month or so in the hospital NICU. You would think life could not get any worse, right? Bringing this baby home was another challenge for our family dynamic, but I found a blessing in everything even when it looked the worst.

We all had to adjust to his medical challenges. Many

days he had to be hospitalized. We were blessed with a home-care nurse who would come into our home and attend to his needs all day. God bless Auntie Grace, as my children called Dominion's nurse. Her skills and knowledge and care towards my baby boy cannot be compared. I will forever be grateful to her. I was out on maternity leave and relied on that check to help with financial expenses, but eventually that resource ran out. Trying to pay the rent on the first of the month became difficult, but I paid it. It was late, but it was paid in full.

Even though we paid the rent, late but faithfully, the landlord decided she wanted us out. So, she dragged us to court under false pretenses saying that we weren't paying any rent at all. The back and forth to court added more strain to our already challenging life. Each month she collected a late rent, she would take me to court the following week or so. But I was determined to keep a roof over my family's head. After a few months, the landlord came and demanded that we leave the apartment. Here I was with a medically challenged baby, my husband withering away emotionally, mentally, and physically right in front of my eyes, and she was putting us out in the cold.

Her demand was so cruel. Even though the judge had ruled in our favor every time we went to court, this lady snatched up my belongings and threw them all on the sidewalk giving us a 24-hour warning to leave the property. My heart was so broken as I watched my children screaming and crying at this cruel act. She had no remorse and continued her rampage to ruin my family. I did not have the strength to fight with her. I just stood knowing God would somehow fight for me. This was traumatic for my children and probably will scar them for the rest of their lives.

The following day I had to rush my baby to the hospital where he was admitted once again. My family had been thrown into homelessness again, and my husband's pride made him refuse to ask for help. So, I had to call for help myself. I made a few phone calls and what I had fought the most was now going to be our reality. Right before my eyes my family had to split up. The two older ones went with a church member, and my youngest daughter went with her godmother. Thank God my baby was in the hospital. While Dominion was in the hospital, my husband and I stayed in another county with a family member.

We traveled two hours or more everyday back and forth to the hospital and trying to visit our children all in one day. This was so heartbreaking and a heavy burden. God was all we had, and he promised he would not leave us nor forsake us. I held on to those words hoping he would come through for us soon. I pleaded with God with all the remaining strength I had left. I wanted my family back together, and for the first time I saw their sadness in their eyes every time I stopped to check on them. They didn't say much, but their faces pleaded with me to come home again.

I had no answers for them, but I wanted to have answers not just for them but for me too. It was the lowest place I had ever been. I had no more words, only love. I pleaded with God to bring my family back together, and it was not long before he blessed us with a one-bedroom suite in a hotel. It was big enough for all of us to come back together. We gathered up my children and moved into this hotel suite grateful for the blessing. It was not my townhome, but it was a provision from God so everyone could come back together.

Six weeks had now passed since my baby boy's birth, and it was time for me to go back to work. It was so difficult. I spent days in the bathroom pumping breast milk, and on my lunch break I would travel to the hospital NICU to visit and feed him. I was so grateful the hospital wasn't far, and I was able to make it back to work on time. The cost of living went up again and we had to pay $583 a week to stay in our comfortable one-bedroom suite. Honestly, it was more like an apartment with one bedroom, two beds, a kitchen, a bathroom, and a facility to wash our clothes. It was so much pressure to come up with the money some weeks. When you do the math, we were paying more than what it would've been to rent a one-bedroom apartment.

There were times when the payment was due, and I was not sure how much money I had on my card.

A voice came to me and said, "Swipe the card," and sure enough the payment went through.

I did not have enough praises to give God for such divine favor. As finances drained out, unlike other times I put my pride aside and immediately asked different people for help. Occasionally, some were not able to contribute, and yes, it was so painful. Nevertheless, we kept pressing and I kept asking as needed.

Another painful issue during this time was my husband's sexual drive diminishing. It became frustrating for the both of us. It was always the one thing we were able to keep consistent no matter what we went through. However, with the tremendous amount of stress we had encountered, his heart condition worsened, and he became drastically ill. I was so worried about him and how long he would survive this suffering. Being the anchor for my family was my primary focus, and I couldn't shift my responsibility. I had no choice but to go into overdrive to meet the demands of each role.

The search began for a new place. The sadness of being rejected by every housing complex because of the eviction record attached to my name was so painful and hopeless. No one wanted my family. It was as if we had a plague, and everyone was avoiding us. For this, I became so disappointed and depressed. Walking around with a partial smile on the outside, while bleeding with pain on the inside. I managed to dress up my emotions daily to continue the search for a place of our own, keeping my faith in God as best I could.

Throughout my struggles with depression, God was faithful and assured me through dreams that things would work out for our good in his time. I believe God wanted me to rely solely on him during this time, remembering that he said in his word to come unto him all who are heavy laden, and to cast my cares on him. So, I decided to obey his promises. Eventually I stopped looking for a place, and just asked God to be the master of my emotions. I came to realize that this was spiritual warfare, and if God did not step in and work things out nothing was not going to work. I had to put myself into a place of stillness, and quiet the voices in my head so I could hear him clearly.

After a couple days of being still and resting in God, a dream came to me and God instructed me to re-apply to the same complex that evicted me. Once I did, I would be approved. Now why would God send me back the place that split up my family and broke me so badly? The dark demons of negativity strangled my thoughts, and I just could not see that manifestation. Nevertheless, I gathered up my faith and trusted the prophecy of that dream. I put on my bright smile, went to the management office of that complex, and reapplied for another two-bedroom apartment. Just as those dark thoughts told me, I was denied and told I would never ever be eligible to rent any property, especially in that complex.

I was so confused, and in my secret place I questioned God. Obviously, there was a conflict with my dream and the decision rendered. How can I be approved and denied at the same time?

The great thing was our hotel suite had enough space and comfort for everyone, and for that I was grateful. We didn't have to jeopardize our privacy staying with others anymore; and while most of our food supplies came from the local pantry, it was okay because I was back in the kitchen, a place I enjoyed. The children's demeanor had changed to be more relaxed, and even though my baby boy was dealing with health challenges, I knew how to cope.

The one thing that bothered my spirit was if low-budget hotels were a form of shelter for the homeless, why were the families being charged so much? The problem was financial lack in the first place. I mean, whose idea was this to charge a family to live in a shelter? In the end, it was better than the ones we once stayed. One of the sweetest lessons was to know that circumstances did not define me but strengthened me. I also learned to trust God no matter the pain and suffering. Although those lessons came to me after the storm of pain came to a halt, they were still good lessons.

Things were once again getting tight financially, and I didn't know how much longer we'd be able to stay in the hotel. Each family shelter that we applied to refused to take us as an entire family. The rule was the husband had to be excluded from the family and stay in a separate shelter. The thought of separating from my husband was unacceptable to me. There was no way I wanted that form of separation. Well, what was meant for evil in the end God turned it for my family's good.

The eviction notices against me seemed like a dark cloud constantly over my head. Turns out for me to rent at any property from the complex I was evicted, the approval would now be based on the regional office. I went on a fast and prayed, remembering the dream God gave me that I would be approved. It was tiresome, and God knows I wanted a little stability. Praise God! After much review we were accepted back into the system to rent again. The moment of relief was finally upon us. Just the thought of the dark cloud no longer being over my head was much to give God thanks. This approval became the end of our homelessness and instability.

We discovered there was a blessing in the wait. While we were going through the process of having our application reviewed by the regional office, a brand-new complex was being built across from where we were evicted. I applied, and with the divine favor of God we were approved. A new day was on the horizon, and we blessed God for it.

CHAPTER 16

The Turning Tides

In May 2019, we moved into our brand-new apartment. Things were on the rise. This new apartment was triple the size of what we lost and suffered through. Oh, the burden was lifted from everyone. It reflected on the children's faces. Although my baby boy was medically challenged, I believe he felt the freedom too as he ran from room to room just giggling in the purest state. I walked from room to room praising God. The intensity of my praises invoked everyone else to join in, and we all worshipped God together.

Shortly after our move, my husband's mental and physical health started to decline even more. His heart condition worsened at such a speed. Maybe it was all the strain, stress, and pain he took on over the years that was now taking a drastic toll on him. During all his challenges, he was denied disability several times. He couldn't support us the way he wanted to, yet he found ways to still be strong and show his support and love for us.

Just as he did during my time in graduate school, he encouraged me to keep pursuing my dreams. I had a dream to start my own business, and there is no doubt he saw that fruition ahead of me. Sadly, on April 26, 2020, my beloved husband, Elder Douglas Wych, II, suffered a massive heart attack on his way to the bathroom. That day, my husband, my best friend, and my king died without seeing all the gain of our labor.

Earlier that day he snuck out of bed, made breakfast, and served me breakfast in bed. I was so excited to see him in full strength and back to how he used to treat me in our early days of dating and marriage before the children. The day started out beautifully. He went to the children individually and had a heart-to-heart talk with them. He encouraged each one to be the best version of themselves, then prayed over them, and gave them kisses as he told them how much he loved them.

He came back to our room and embraced me with the love burning in his eyes. He reminded me of his love and apologized for not being the man and husband I wanted or that he had promised my dad some years back. The compassion in his eyes touched my heart as we cried together. For sure, I knew he was happy we were now living together in a space I desired. The look on his face was relaxed and assured me that God still had me even though it seemed as if he'd failed me.

A little later in the day, we had an early dinner. We all sat down and ate together, just as we'd normally do. Right after dinner my dear husband asked me to take a walk with him outside, which was unusual. We were in the peak of the COVID-19 pandemic, and he was normally too weak to walk lengthy distances. The thought of him struggling to breathe while wearing a mask with his heart condition was scary, but I was willing to grant him his minor request. It was a sunny Sunday evening, and the temperature was fair. We were not going far because while walking his steps became slower for every two steps.

Being a bit considerate I asked, "Honey we can go back home?"

His response was a simple, "No, I want to walk with you."

So, we continued our walk. I held on to his hand very tight and whispered a quiet prayer for the Lord to grant him just a little more strength. During my prayer, he stopped, looked at me, and stared into my eyes. He gave me a gentle kiss as if he knew it would be our last kiss and walk together. My heart melted as if it was the first time we kissed. It reminded me of when we used to go on dates with a sense of shyness and love combined.

I was glad he took the time to get outside and go on this small walk which was probably five minutes but seemed longer at his slow pace. We headed back in the house and I joined a church service online while my husband went to rest. While praying, I saw a clear vision of my husband having a heart attack. Within a minute of that vision and getting off the service I heard a loud crashing sound echo in my ears. There was no crying from any of my children, but I dashed to my bedroom to find my husband laid out just a couple steps from the bathroom door. The pain of seeing him struck me cold and sent me into an unconscious state for a second. There was no time to panic as I called out to Majesty to help me.

Upon Majesty's arrival, I grabbed the phone to make that terrible call to 911 to say my husband may be having a massive heart attack. It became so real in that quick moment of the operator answering.

"911, what's your emergency?"

As the operator instructed me to do CPR, my son and I took turns performing it, but there was no response. A short time later, the EMTs showed up and continued CPR as well as other procedures. The words rung in my ears as the EMT spoke.

"I'm so sorry."

They pronounced him dead right before my very eyes while my first-born son stood by my side.

Just like that the clouds returned over my head on that bright Sunday evening at the height of a worldwide pandemic as I kissed my husband of 18 years goodbye and became a widow with four children.

Nevertheless, in the words of my husband's favorite

song, "God had been too good to me, and I wasn't going to complain."

We often sang that song together during our struggles. God will definitely answer your "whys" even when they don't look right to you. I kept trusting God even though this moment of death was hard to swallow. Somewhere in it, God's promises to me remained.

How can I not acknowledge God as my divine healer in his forever faithfulness? It was my pain that caused me to trust God regardless of what was going on around me. It was my praise, oh yes, my praise that allowed me to endure my pain. It is my praise that reminds me of the many roads I have traveled, and the miracles that God did on each one of them. I am a miracle, a promise filled with possibilities established long before I was conceived in my mother's womb. It is clear that after all the diagnosis among myself and my family, the pain and suffering we have endured, God is not through with us yet. I stand on my prayers and praise knowing God, The Almighty, The Great Creator, will do that which he said he would do.

Doug had persuaded me to apply for my Doctorate degree a few months prior to his passing, but because of all our family challenges, I decided to apply for online courses so I could be home with my family. Although he is not here with me anymore, I still have a choice to vibrate higher with his knowledge and love while I raise our children. As we stood at his graveside shedding tears, I made a promise that I would enjoy every moment with them on his behalf. There is no doubt in my heart that whatever knowledge and wisdom he deposited in them early that Sunday morning would leave a lasting impact on their lives. My baby boy Dominion who was turning three the following month spent the next couple days asking for "daddy." I am confident somewhere in his little heart he was assured by God that his daddy went away, but his spirit will be watching over him as he never asked for his daddy again. However, I know not seeing his father every time he enters the room will be a question to answer when he grows up.

The outstanding dedication he had towards his family, even through illness, will allow me to celebrate each day as if it is a birthday celebration, especially during the times we are challenged with his absence. I am grateful to have my children with me, and each day they teach me the true meaning of life. I see my husband's traits shining through them, and it is a solid reminder that his spirit is still with me no matter where I go in life. There was so much we wanted to do together. Now that I stand as a widow, I must go on and complete the task with my head lifted to The Almighty God. I can only go forward from here.

CHAPTER 17

The Revelation

Through sickness, lack, and homelessness, we fought hard to keep our family together and never be separated. I am grateful to God that before my husband left us God saw to it that we were not only reunited, but that provisions were in place for us. Today I rise out of the dirt of homelessness and lack. God has blessed me with an overflow. I have freedom, peace of mind, my health, and my children, but most importantly I have joy, Heavenly joy, and strength to carry on into my destiny.

Looking back, oh I miss the days of my childhood. They were filled with such joy.

I'm glad God kept me, and am proud to say, "I would not trade my childhood for nothing in this world."

Can you say that about your childhood? If not, I hope by reading my story you are able to see a light of hope and strength to create your future. Although we cannot go back into our childhood, we can learn from every stage of those years and apply what we've learned to our present and future. With humility and peace, how I felt about the investment of my parents defined every moment and decision I made going forward. Parents, I hope you will be inspired to add the best of joy and happiness to your children's childhood so they will grow up with pure motivation and desire to build on your legacy.

All the suffering I endured allowed me to realize that I am called out and ordained a prophet for the Lord from the foundation of the world. Jeremiah 1:5 reads, "Before I formed you in the womb I knew[a] you, before you were born I set you apart; I appointed you as a prophet to the nations." While going through my sufferings, I gained all my answers of how to maneuver through the struggles through prophetic utterance from the Lord through dreams and visions. In turn, my faith and obedience to what was revealed to me was my road map to deliverance and peace of mind. It's one thing to believe God when he speaks to you, but to put action to what he says is something different.

Proverbs 3:5-6 reads, "Trust in the LORD with all your heart and do not lean on your own understanding. In all your ways acknowledge Him and he will direct your path." My pain brought me to a place of trusting in the Lord with not a part of my heart, but all my heart and I did not lean to my own understanding. While going through I was determined to trust God every step of the way! I knew I was my family's hope to get through homelessness and the sickness of my husband, even while dealing with my own infirmities. To get through the storm, I was the key to their growth and development to know that God is a deliverer.

From my pain I gained strength, during what felt like my weakest days. I remained in the posture of prayer and worship. When I was weak, I didn't give up. I learned to pray even more. I learned to laugh when I wanted to cry and remained faithful in being kind to God's people. I still managed to minister to others through my brokenness, even while dealing with breast cancer. I gained a dimension of praise that was unorthodox.

My praise took me into the spiritual realm and a higher dimension I had never experienced before. It became my weapon against severe depression and mental breakdowns. I realized that praise was comely for the upright (Psalms 33:1), so my praise got turned into a daily routine in my household. As a result of my praise to God, I gained stamina to continue my process and journey chains of depression, anxiety, and weariness were broken off me and my family. Yes, praise was my chain breaker. "And at midnight Paul and Silas prayed, and sang praises unto God: and the prisoners heard them. And suddenly there was a great earthquake, so that the foundations of the prison were shaken: and suddenly all the doors were opened, and every one's bands were loosed." - Acts 16:25-26

Lastly one unknown author said, "Healing doesn't mean the damage never existed. It means the damage no longer controls our lives."

Therefore, I refuse to let my past wounds frighten me out of my destiny and purpose. Through it all I learned how to endure and embrace who God is in my life. I have come to the full understanding of my authentic self and my designed purpose on this Earth. That purpose is to serve others in fullness and truth, and be a change agent for The Almighty God, walking in his image. After all that I went through I am proud to say I am now a prayer warrior, business owner, and now an author.

On November 17, 2020 at 5:09 A.M., the Holy Ghost gave me these words, "In order to know your gifts and talents, you have to be conscious of who you are."

My advice to you is to discover your gifts and talents and learn how to become conscious of who you really are. Today my love for the underprivileged has increased immensely, and I pray to gain enough to give back to the less fortunate one day. My dream is to help them gain that which they have lost and revive their dreams from the ashes. I never gave up on God or his promise, and because of that I can write this story to inspire someone else not to give up.

There were many times I could have just laid there and died to all the struggles and buried myself in shame. But

God had a different plan not only for me, but my family. We must remember there is a path we all have to travel. While we are on it, we must seek our purpose and do our best to fulfill it. What I gained is not about materialistic acquisitions. It is about finding peace in it all and knowing my purpose. Understand, pain is a part of the process, and without it there is no gain. Nobody ever told us about the pain or even gave us a small hint on how to deal with it. We had to develop those skills and fight to survive.

Let's discover our purpose and authentic self. Your pain does not define you, but it will shape and point you in the direction of your destiny! Remember, fight with an end result in mind, and know you are never alone.

"I will never leave you nor forsake you, saith the Lord."
Deuteronomy 31:6

ABOUT THE AUTHOR

AVIS WILLIS

Avis Willis was born in Jamaica, West Indies, but God had a special calling on her life that extended far beyond the Caribbean borders. In 1990, she moved with her mother and one of her sisters from Jamaica to the Bronx, New York, where they joined her father and three older siblings. Upon arrival in the United States, she attended school in the New York Public School System.

Despite growing up in poverty, Avis persevered through the hard-core living of the "Boogie Down Bronx" and strives for excellence in all her pursuits. In 1998 she obtained a Bachelor's degree in Social Sciences from Niagara University and, in 2000, a Master's degree in Social work from Howard University.

Avis was ordained as an Evangelist and has served in the capacity of a District Missionary and Co-Pastor during her ministerial career. Throughout the year, she can be found in the Caribbean or the United States ministering as a Prayer Revivalist.

She is the widow of the late Elder Douglas Wych, II and the mother of their four beautiful children. Currently in pursuit of her Doctorate in Social Work, Avis is indeed an anointed "chosen vessel" of God. She is determined to fulfill her God-given assignment and to live a holy life in this present world.

www.ingramcontent.com/pod-product-compliance
Lightning Source LLC
Chambersburg PA
CBHW071848070526
44583CB00016B/1601